Fairy Tales

Joanne Larby

A glittering guide to surviving with sparkle

BLACKWATER PRESS

Acknowledgements

Thank you to my publisher John O'Connor for believing in my vision and having faith in a fairy. Thank you to the editorial and design team at Blackwater Press for being at the end of the line no matter what my query was, bringing my dream to life and keeping me calm whilst working with me on the final stages of this book.

To my photographer and friend Tiara Rad for capturing the moments that make up this book. For knowing my angles and making me look and feel my best. To Gavin Monaghan for providing the perfect professional lighting and assistance.

To my illustrator Momna Aakel for knowing exactly what I wanted creatively right down to every last detail.

To my fashion designer Fi Bourke for creating the most magical yet mature fairy costume for the cover of this book.

To my stylist Clémentine Mac Neice for taking me out of my comfort zone and putting together a wardrobe of looks that worked so well together.

To my skilled make up artist Hazel Ward who took the pressure off, meaning I could relax and enjoy our intense two-day shoot.

Thank you to my nail girl Sarah Gaynor for making sure my manicure was on point.

A massive thank you to my personal trainer Stephen Kenny-Gains for working out with me, giving me constant advice and contributing to the fitness section of this book.

Thank you to my fabulous family, who have always believed in my decisions and direction, for putting up with someone trapped in her room writing for the past few months and for always supporting me spreading my wings. A special thank you to mama fairy, who continues to act as my rock and inspiration in life, without you I wouldn't be me. Thank you for being my second editor, and reading through my work every step of the way. Also thank you to my brother, for understanding why his sister takes so many selfies and for putting up with my online presence even though he probably gets stick from the lads for it.

To my fabulous friends, who are always around to lend a hand or an ear, to share my success and celebrate each and every triumph. For taking countless outfit pictures on nights out and never tiring of having a fairy for a friend.

Thank you to my furry friend and family dog Snipe, for being there for a cuddle in between stressful moments on all those manic days working from home, alone, when I wanted to give up.

And finally, to my followers, without whom this simply wouldn't be possible. For every interaction and well wish, for watching my daily life, for attending my workshops and master classes, for growing with me as a woman and for being a positive light on the darkest days.

Contents

Introduction

When I was a little girl my head was filled with fairies and fantasy, I had burning glitter running through my veins and frantically sketched unicorns in my spare time. My bedroom was a haven and outlet for creativity, thankfully my equally artistic mum allowed me use my interior space as a form of expression. From themed wall paintings to clothing alterations I was a creative little soul. Aside from all things girly, I was a deep thinker and a regular ear to council my friends.

Fast forward some years and I had completed a course in Art College, followed by Make Up Artistry, and studied Montessori, Special Needs and Child Psychology.

At the age of 25 I became my own boss and created the brand The Make Up Fairy. What initially began as a blogging hobby, which I used as a means to grow my name as a make up artist while I worked as a teacher, fast became one of Ireland's biggest beauty brands.

This book brings together my experiences as an entrepreneur, blogger, model and woman.

I regularly share my body confidence secrets while I work as an active curvy model, create written and video content online, teach my followers the top tips and tricks of the trade, hold beauty and style workshops and social media seminars around Ireland, review hotel stays in the travel section of my website, collaborate with big name brands worldwide and offer advice. When I first began, my mum was probably my only fan and follower and now I have a combined social media following of over 120,000 people which is growing all the time, have been voted by *Vogue Italia* as the top curvy girl in the world to follow, I've won awards such as Best Company Beauty Blog and Best Social Media in Ireland, and been nominated for awards in international magazines like *Cosmopolitan*. I've worked as the social media ambassador and videographer for the likes of L'Oréal and Easilocks, as the beauty blogger for some of the main department stores in Ireland and featured in a myriad of TV shows and print media.

The more my following expands the more private mails I receive daily from women around the world, telling me how much I inspire them to carve their own career paths, love their bodies, become fit and healthy, manage their anxiety and even break out of unhealthy relationships. At this point in my career I feel like somewhat of a fairy godmother to my online following. It is a position I take very seriously, and as such I wanted to create something that would house all the information I've been bursting to share for so long. From building a business and banishing blemishes to surviving stress, panic attacks and heart break, this book encapsulates the struggles we face as women breaking into a harsh and saturated industry and includes advice on the exterior emotional situations we all encounter, with a tongue in cheek twist.

The most amazing part about my job is the ability to interact with my followers daily, so this book combines my ideas with your suggestions to ensure every area and topic is covered.

As a beauty and lifestyle blogger I spend my day writing content for my own website and other media outlets, so publishing a book was always a natural progression and long-term dream of mine. I didn't want this book to be a basic beauty bible or simple style guide; I wanted to bring everything my brand embodies into one *glittering guide to surviving with sparkle*. I want you to be able to indulge in my humble success story, turn negative life situations into positive progress and above all feel empowered. Whether you're a loyal fairy follower or someone who picked up this book from a shop shelf out of intrigue, I wrote this for you and believe in you.

Chapter **1**

Website
Wonder

Beautiful Background

When I was a tiny tot my mum dressed me in the most girly of attire. From hair ties that matched the bows on my socks to frilly vests and pink polka dot shoes, I was the epitome of feminine.

As a single parent, Mama Fairy worked hard to maintain a lovely lifestyle for us both and ensured I wanted for nothing. By the time I turned three, she had built her own property on my granddad's land and we shared our first Christmas together in our new home complete with a hot pink tree and tacky baubles. I have nothing but fond memories of our relationship and we're still the best of friends to this day. A talented actress, she instilled independence and confidence in me throughout my upbringing and taught me that the only way to have anything in life is to go out and get it. My aunty was also a big influence when I was younger. Living next door to us, she spent a huge amount of time looking after me and generally helping out while mum was working. When I was five-and-a-half years old, mum met my step-father through a drama production they were both working on. Shortly after, he moved in with us and they had my brother. I was ecstatic; finally a sibling to share my time with. He was quite literally a bundle of joy. Innocent, with chubby cheeks, and full of giggles, I was proud of the fact that I was the first person ever to make him laugh as a baby. Although there was a seven-year age-gap between us, we were extremely close and I suited the big sister role. He has since grown into a very handsome and intelligent man and I'm increasingly proud of his achievements.

He was quite literally a bundle of joy. Innocent, with chubby cheeks, and full of giggles...

Strengths and Weaknesses

The men in our household are pragmatic and factual which is balanced by the emotional, sensitive souls of my mum and I. Like most families, our skill sets and desires in life are quite contrasting and my brother and I approached school and college very differently to each other.

I was always terrible at Maths and hated Physics. Numbers stressed my thought process and I marvelled at people who actually liked algebra. Instead, I excelled at subjects such as Art and Languages and put all of my efforts into my creative mindset. My principal suggested to my parents that I should be a lawyer with my innate ability to convince others black was white during debates in English class. I lived for Art class, thoroughly enjoyed speaking French and happily spent hours working on essay assignments. I gave up ballet and gymnastics when I hit secondary school but remained somewhat sporty, dabbling in hockey, athletics, swimming and horse-riding. I have relatively positive memories of education and school was a social time for me, I reached my peak at around fifth year when I made a few friends for life. When exam time came I was a little too social; I spent more time with said friends than I did studying. I knew I had the ability to get considerably high marks in my Leaving Cert but much to my own detriment I focused on my favourite subjects, ensuring I got straights A's in those instead of working on my weak areas. The result was a fairly decent collation of points that signified I did just fine but reminded me I could have done better.

My Study Journey

After completing my Leaving Cert I was torn between studying Journalism, Fashion Design or Make Up Artistry. I loved the English language and putting my thoughts on paper but worried about the immediate job opportunities after completing the course if I studied Journalism.

When it came to Fashion Design, I had a great sense of style and interest in trends but the four-year course seemed like such a long time to not be working and earning and all the while Make Up Artistry remained at the forefront of my mind. To try and appease my indecision I decided to

complete a portfolio course first to collate a mixture of skills including sketching, painting and sculpture and then decide which avenue I wanted to explore. I found every area enjoyable and therapeutic and realised my niche was definitely on the creative spectrum. I met a great group of like-minded individuals on the portfolio course and thoroughly enjoyed my time delving into imaginative projects. Just like in secondary school, the art class environment was calming and I felt at home. Whether we were on a day trip to the Botanic Gardens to paint still life or practising graphic design, creating posters and working on logos, every aspect appealed to me. At the end of the year after researching various courses I applied for Theatrical Media And Make Up Artistry, which was one year full time and included every area of make up. I was eager to begin work as soon as possible and gradually up-skill while I earned, which I considered ideal.

> *I found every area enjoyable and therapeutic and realised my niche was definitely on the creative spectrum.*

Making It

Throughout the year-long, full time course at Senior College Dun Laoghaire I worked on generic areas of study, the theory of artistry including anatomy and physiology, skin diseases and disorders, high fashion and catwalk looks, basic beauty therapy, advanced artistry including wig-making, bald caps, bruises, abrasions and even theatrical prosthetics.

Another positive college experience, I adored every minute of the course and excelled in every area receiving top marks in all of my exams. I had discovered my calling amongst a group of girly girls and immediately knew I had made the right decision. The qualifications I received meant I was able to work abroad as a recognised artist and simply had to decide if I wanted to go down the fashion or theatrical route. Although I'm in awe of the work created by MUA's in the likes of *Lord Of The Rings,* basic wounds and media artistry in Ireland didn't appeal to me. The chances of making it big were slim and the money was poor. I had a keen eye for style and I was still eager to explore my passion for fashion, so I decided to start my CV with some beauty counter work. At the end of my exams I began applying for jobs and ended up working with Shiseido for two years. Predominantly a skincare brand, they also have an extensive make up line so I was able to practise everything I had worked on in college from facials to application. I was also lucky enough to work freelance as the Shiseido MUA and booked jobs for the *Sunday World* magazine and *RTÉ Guide* during my time there. After working with the world-renowned skincare brand I wanted to move to a younger brand that put more focus on artistry. I ended up with Smashbox for a similar length of time and adored my time with the LA line. I up-skilled quickly, learning

how to manage my time and I even accrued regular clients who then started to book me outside work hours, in turn growing my freelance name. I was also busy looking after retail selling, targets, managerial paperwork, stock take, brand expansions and delegation.

From Student to Teacher

At this point of my career I felt I had enough retail experience, I had worked with a myriad of different faces and product lines, I had built up an extensive portfolio of credited jobs, which meant my name and work had appeared in a variety of print media, I continued to work freelance on shoots, fine-tuned my timing and gained lots of loyal customers.

My options for advancement were to either apply for an area manager job and travel as a make up artist or go freelance which I was loath to do due to the instability and lack of set salary.

I decided I was ready to dive into another area of education I was passionate about while still maintaining my freelance work.

I decided I was ready to dive into another area of education I was passionate about while still maintaining my freelance work. Although they're wildly different to the superficial world of make up, child care and psychology were areas I had a huge interest in but it wasn't until I had immersed myself in every area of art that I realised I still needed to fill a void. I wanted to study again, to test my brain and challenge myself, I wanted to work on something more meaningful and that's exactly what I did. I immersed myself in child care and the world of Maria Montessori. I fell in love with the entire educational approach which was characterised by an emphasis on respect, independence, freedom within limits and a child's natural psychological, physical, and social development.

I was fascinated by the scientific pedagogy and researched constantly outside college hours. I spent long nights compiling immaculate teaching files and received straight A's in every exam. After studying Montessori, Child Psychology and Special Needs I was now a qualified teacher. I luckily landed myself a job in the private school where I did my work experience and spent three fabulous years looking after two daily classes filled with beautiful boys and girls aged 2-5. I adored my time as a teacher and felt immediately at home in the nurturing environment. From parent teacher meetings to graduation day and all of the regular teaching days in between, I fell in love with every child I worked with and ended up becoming a nanny after school hours for two families. While I was working as a teacher I continued to work as a make up artist during the evenings and at weekends and wanted to make both of my business ventures successes.

Building a Brand

After deciding to work towards making a business out of all the career areas I had explored, I needed a name. I wanted something catchy and unique that signified what my brand was about, included the service I could provide and had a deeper meaning than meets the eye.

I always loved fantasy as a child and regularly sketched mythical creatures, mainly fairies. Make up was the base of my business so joining the two together seemed perfect. Just like a dream come true, I carried over some of the things I had loved as a child and merged them together with all the things I had learned as an adult. The Make Up Fairy represents everything girly and embodies positivity. The term 'make up' can mean to revamp or change for the better,

whether it's switching up your style or learning how to apply a smoky eye. It can also mean forgiveness, mending an argument or to improve for the better. The brand was never going to be simply superficial; I wanted to showcase my skills as an artist but also utilise my background in psychology to actually help people. In essence I was living two very different lives that were joined together by one passion. Whether it was making a woman feel more beautiful in my client chair or offering advice online, this was a sparkle service with a difference. A fairy generally carries a wand with her and my idea was to replace the wand with a make up brush to make my choice of logos and branding really stand out. I started to sketch some rough ideas of what I had in mind and the colour scheme I wanted to go for. I was the face of my brand and the fairy so I simply had to adapt my attire, add some wings, my wand of choice and the brand was born. I enjoyed the variety this created in my day, from teaching a child to read his first word to heading home to my new hobby and project, I felt fulfilled and every plan started falling into place.

Online Outlet

Starting a blog was an obvious choice for me. I read blogs daily, following fashionistas online, enjoyed writing and sharing my feelings, and knew I needed to get my name out there.

At the time I had a personal Facebook page but I was aware I had to somewhat segregate my personal life from my business, so I made a Facebook Like Page, Instagram, Twitter, Pinterest and YouTube accounts all under The Make Up Fairy name. The next stage was creating a website. I had no idea how to start a blog, in fact around the time I started, blogging was a much smaller community than it is now and certain social media outlets like Instagram were just starting to become popular. I called up my friend Donal Skehan, a hugely talented and successful author, and all-round entrepreneur in the food industry, who essentially made his name online through a blog, and asked him for help. He advised me that I had to purchase a domain name and then begin writing content on either Blogger or WordPress. We both agreed that although my brand would be The Make Up Fairy, I needed to think about down the line when my brand matured and I became well known. Would I want to be known as a fairy or just Joanne? Even then I was thinking big. After some time and thought I purchased the domain name www.joannelarby.com and made a Blogger account. I spent the first week or so playing around with the layout of my page, the colour scheme, adding a banner and tweaking the text appearance. When I was content I started to plan my home page. Make up, Beauty, Fashion and Decor were my core headers to house my content. The make up section would include tutorials and step-by-step guides on application, the beauty section would cover product reviews and new launches, fashion would allow me to showcase my own personal style and what I purchased and decor was anything and everything from interior design inspiration to card making.

Finding My Niche

I wanted my blog to appeal to a wide audience from young girly girls all the way up to more mature women. I also wanted to ensure my content was varied so that a future follower who didn't like make up would perhaps enjoy the body confidence advice I had to offer or vice versa.

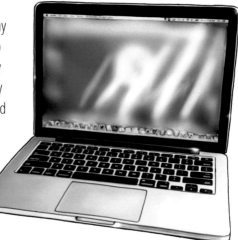

When I first began writing articles my audience was my mum; no one else knew The Make Up Fairy existed so social media was my tool for sharing my feed. Every day I would update my social media profiles with beauty and style imagery, funny memes, inspiring quotes and consistent content. Even though I had a minuscule audience I made sure my updates were regular and people knew when to expect a new blog post. I had a very clear vision and believed that this was going to eventually work and my efforts would pay off. Within a few weeks I was contacted by my first ever PR company and sent some deodorant to give away. I was literally over the moon and flabbergasted by how they found me online, happy they liked my content and honoured to host a competition.

Another few weeks in and my site statistics began to grow rapidly. The more the figures grew the more passionate I became and the more content I produced. I was still working full time as a teacher at this point so my blog became a hobby I would look forward to working on after a long day. I spent every spare minute blogging or researching and continued to do freelance make up jobs in the evenings and at weekends. The more my name grew online the more bookings I received, the more bookings I got the more my name grew online. I started to work with some UK celebrities and the more they tweeted about my make up magic the more followers I received. The domino effect of hard work and consistency was a magic combination that made The Make Up Fairy more in demand. At this point I was working seven days a week with very little free time but I loved every minute of it and the burning fire and ambition continued to grow.

Making It as a Model

I've always had a curvy frame with big boobs and bum; even when I was slim I had an hourglass shape. I assumed by virtue of my physique that I would never be suitable for modelling. Plus size modelling didn't really exist at the time in Ireland and I didn't want to get skinny or change myself dramatically, so I began modelling on my own blog, which seemed to be a perfect solution.

I had a passion for fashion and a keen eye for bargain buys so I began taking photos of my daily outfits, which included mirrored images standing back-to-back, close up detail shots of my accessories and links to purchase everything I was wearing. Soon to be my signature OOTD (outfit of the day) posts, my poses became more practised and polished and I gained a new army of fellow curvy followers. People would comment, commending me on how I pieced high and low end items together and how they loved the fact that I embraced my fuller figure. I received an email from *U* magazine asking to do a fashion diary piece, which would include a day in the life of Joanne Larby. Over the moon, I contacted a photographer I had worked with previously on a make up shoot, Dermot Byrne and pulled clothes for the piece from Ted Baker, FCUK and Zara. We shot twelve key looks showcasing my signature style in various locations around Dublin and sent off the professional images. After the feature went to print I was signed by Assets Model Agency as a plus size model and lots of readers wrote in to the magazine saying how nice and refreshing it was to witness a woman who loved her lumps and bumps. And so my modelling career began. I walked in catwalk shows from bridal to lingerie, featured in various newspaper and magazine style features and TV slots. I continued to model my own wardrobe on the blog and took lots of behind the scenes images on location while I was working. My Montessori school was very understanding and allowed me switch my hours if I had a TV gig in the morning but my schedule was becoming increasingly difficult to juggle.

Difficult Decisions

In my final year teaching, the long hours that I was putting into blogging and modelling essentially meant that I was working two jobs and becoming progressively more tired and somewhat stressed.

I was extremely happy and comfortable working in Montessori and loved every minute of my job, but the creative business career I had essentially been trying to build since leaving school was finally starting to really take off. My days consisted of cycling to work for 8am, exhausted,

looking after a morning session of 15 kids, breaking for lunch where I would catch up on social media and work on my website, looking after an afternoon session of 7 kids, collecting the kids from the two families I worked for, working as a nanny until around 7pm, cycling home, grabbing a quick bite to eat, walking my two dogs or spending time with my then-boyfriend, getting ready to attend an event to network, posting a tutorial of my make up online, taking outfit imagery, coming home to edit said imagery and blogging. Some mornings were spent modelling on TV, some evenings were spent doing make up trials and debs make up, and weekends were spent teaching make up lessons, getting people ready for parties, maintaining a three-bedroom house, and working on the website or upcoming interviews.

I was beyond burning the candle at both ends and knew a big decision was impending; would I remain teaching or give The Make Up Fairy a go full time? After weeks of wondering what to do, speaking with friends, family and my boss, I decided to leave my job as a teacher before Christmas with the intent to return at a later stage in my life. My qualifications would always stand to me and the school staff fully supported my decision, agreeing that everything was taking off for me and I was at the perfect age to begin building my own business. Worst case scenario, I could return to my teaching job doing the odd freelance nixer, best case scenario I could make it successfully as a boss, working my own hours, choosing my daily grind and become well-known for my talents on a much larger scale.

Branching Out on My Own

After handing in my notice I began making a plan of action. I contacted a web designer about turning my blog into an official website with improved functionality and an online magazine feel.

The conversion was no easy task because we had to move hundreds of articles from a Blogger format to WordPress without losing any of my work. I wanted additional tabs and apps added to allow for an online store and planned to change the entire layout and design. The next step was to source my inspiration for the new layout and theme for my website. This was the fun part, considering I had been thinking about the colours and design for such a long time and each component carried it's own significance to provide individuality. I used to wake up at night and put pen to paper, my mind bursting with ideas and details. For the colour scheme I chose a four colour palette including the perfect peach, powder pink, tiffany turquoise and silver sparkle. Peach is a colour I've always loved and worn, I find it compliments tanned skin and it was the colour of my first knitted jumper as a baby. Powder pink signifies the ultimate girly shade and represents every little princess out there. Tiffany turquoise is my favourite blue hue

and symbolises elegance and luxury by virtue of the jewellery brand. Silver sparkle is an accent colour used in less obvious detailed parts of the site to add a gorgeous glitter that subtly stands out. It's like an accessory to my outfit and that touch of sparkle that makes The Make Up Fairy special. The colour palette was also a natural and more mature progression from the original hot pink and teal scheme I used in my initial blog. The colours combined gave a girly yet quirky appearance with class and individuality. After weeks of back and forth fine tuning shades and tweaking things until my web designer wanted to tear my hair extensions out, The Make Up Fairy website was looking far more professional. The next step was completing the rebrand. I contacted a graphic designer and had a banner, logo and social media icons made using matching colour accents and mini make up pots to make my buttons stand out. I had a costume designer create a fairy ensemble, coincidentally the same designer who created the costume on the cover of this book, and had a fun photo shoot to capture some new imagery. The next step was business cards, pull up banners, a launch party and fresh content.

The colour palette was also a natural and more mature progression from the original hot pink and teal scheme I used in my initial blog.

Creating Video Content

After revamping the website I wanted to integrate a YouTube channel to vary the types of content I was offering my audience, considering I had a substantial amount of articles already written and ready to go once the site went live.

I had followed beauty gurus online and admired various channels and editing skills and figured if they could do it so could I. I invested in a good quality camera that I still use today for blog imagery and filming; the Canon DSLR 650D is perfect if you're looking for a tool that will excel in both areas. I had no inclination of how difficult videography would be; from getting your lighting and focus perfect to uploading files that often become corrupted, to using iMovie for completing projects. I spent roughly a week making my first three-minute video and became frustrated at how time-consuming the whole ordeal was, almost giving up on the idea. After plenty of practice and perseverance I became more proficient, and can now make a movie from the starting point to the export in half a day. I wanted my channel to feature mainly quick and easy tutorials, with the odd style video for good measure.

Just like with my blog posts, I was consistent with my uploads, making two videos a week. Within a month my content was recognised by Stylehaul, a network in America, and I was made YouTube partner. Overjoyed, I put even more effort into my channel and have now collated a library of over 120 videos. My time is more precious nowadays so my channel has taken a back seat but my subscribers are still growing daily and I thoroughly enjoy making movies when I find the time. I feel chatty hauls and FAQ tags are a brilliant way to get your personality across and step-by-step tutorials are a great way to showcase your skill set. I ensured my web designer integrated a specific section on my site where people could view my videos and added each finished product thumbnail to my gallery. Now, instead of sending on my portfolio or Media Kit, new companies can view my work for themselves and then contact me through the forum section or various social media outlets, meaning I am consistently advertising my work and brand in a natural way.

My First Big Bash

After a year of running my business I wanted to have a major celebration to acknowledge my own achievement and also to thank my followers for allowing my business to exist and grow.

I decided to call my celebration Fairy First Birthday and to say it was a success is a severe understatement; 700 of my readers arrived in their finest fashion to celebrate in style. According to onlookers, the queue on Grafton Street began at 6pm while fairy followers waited patiently

in the cold until 7.30pm to meet The Make Up Fairy, in fact the Gardaí were even called to see what was going on. Held in Lillie's Bordello, considered Dublin's most renowned and prestigious nightclub, it was my first time running an event from scratch

with little or no experience. The contacts I had built up through blogging were invaluable at the time. In terms of decorations, I had a pink balloon column with an overflowing champagne bottle which was perfect for taking pictures in front of. For entertainment I organised a band and a DJ to keep things varied and appropriate for all guests.

The next step was deciding what to wear. I opted for a floor length lime green gown by designer Rachel Gilbert, which complemented my post-holiday tan nicely. I wanted to display some spectacular food that looked and tasted amazing, so I had a massive edible display made which contained a Make Up Fairy laptop, Tiffany box, card, phone, make up brushes, invitations and shoes on my main cake and added lots of girly toppings and logos to my cupcakes which everyone admired on the night. For the ultimate treat I also wanted some sort of display stand with nibbles and girly decorations. I hired a custom-designed, hand-crafted candy cart to complement the theme and colour scheme of my Fairy First Birthday and added some amazing personal touches, stocked with sweets and treats which were devoured on the night.

I also wanted a pamper stall so I organised a crystal nail bar and glam squad to offer mini manicures and 'a touch of diamond' designs for any of my guests who wanted to feel like a princess on the night. I hired a press call photographer to ensure we had lots of fabulous memories and images that landed in local papers to get further exposure.

Helping Hands

The night before Fairy First Birthday, my family and friends helped me pack 450 goodie bags that contained the most fabulous fillers from make up, hair, and beauty brands to nails and sweet treats from companies I had contacted weeks before.

Alongside the goodie bags I was also sent some amazing prizes for a raffle on the night in order to help raise some much needed money for my chosen charity. Having a charity involved on the night was hugely important to me. I opted for the Make A Wish Foundation who have one simple aim; to

grant the wishes of children aged between 3 and 17 years old, living with life-threatening medical conditions and to enrich the human experience with hope, strength and joy. When I worked on counter as a make up artist, we often worked alongside this foundation providing make overs for their Princess For A Day events, which both touched my heart and left a lasting impression. We raised €1000 on the night thanks to those who bought raffle tickets and a kind donation from Lillie's Bordello. The whole night was a brilliant blur; I managed to meet and interact with every reader there who had supported me throughout my first year in business, which was rather magical. The night also proved I had a flair for organisation and event management and the stresses I experienced still stand to me to this day when pulling workshops together.

Believing in Yourself

The past two years have been pretty spectacular to say the least. My business has expanded from being a basic blog to an online magazine with over 200,000 international readers visiting weekly, a following that grows daily, and brand collaborations with some of the biggest names in the business.

I've become an ambassador for various companies, the beauty editor for major department stores, held master classes and meet and greets around Ireland and even devised my own Make Up Artistry course which I held once a month in Cork last year. I'm signed to three International modelling agencies, have become partner and affiliate to some world-renowned brand names, created my own line of earrings and dresses, and devised my own social media seminar. I've won awards that have included the Best Social Media in the beauty industry and I've been voted one of the Top 6 people to follow in the world by *Vogue Italia*. I'm sent the most amazing products daily, get to wear the most wonderful wardrobe, I'm treated like a celebrity in salons and regularly review luxurious hotel stays. I've also battled with anxiety and panic attacks, I'm a pathological worrier, I'm a painful perfectionist and I've lost relationships as a result of my drive and ambition. My line of work has intimidated and put men off, I've had sleepless nights stressing and been overdrawn in my bank account more times than I can count. I've had to borrow money from my parents when invoices due weren't paid and I was my own accountant for two years, and for someone who's terrible at maths, let me tell you that was a severe struggle. I've met so many amazing people, some of whom are now friends for life. I've also met nasty, vile creatures who have used me up and spat me out. I've learned to figure things out alone and to know when it's time to ask for help. I've been a control freak, and I've lost all control. I've watched things fall apart and witnessed everything coming together to this amazing moment.

Never Give Up

After reading about my journey I hope you can take inspiration and appreciate the reality of chasing your dream job from hearing about my experiences.

Success certainly doesn't happen overnight and it took the guts of six years to combine all of the skills I learned in college, including three different courses, various roles, working two jobs at a time, blood, sweat and plenty of tears to get to where I am today. Put simply, there's no short cut to accomplishing anything in life. If you have a clear and concise vision in your head you have to be willing to sacrifice a huge amount to make what you imagine a reality, you can't give up one year in and wonder why you never made it. I've been stuck in that dead end job, I've questioned was there more to life, I've experienced struggling to pay rent on a low salary, my relationships have suffered, I've said no to countless nights out in a bid to put in extra hours to make this dream work. I've felt temporarily uninspired and then beyond driven the following day, and questioned if any of it was worth the massive highs and lows. The saying 'nothing worth having comes easy' is pretty fitting here. If your dream job was handed to you without any effort you would immediately lack appreciation and have no memory of the grind it usually takes to accomplish something so very rewarding.

If you have a clear and concise vision in your head you have to be willing to sacrifice a huge amount to make what you imagine a reality, you can't give up one year in and wonder why you never made it.

I've learned so much over the years, I've gone from working as part of a large department store team, to a small staffing in a family-run business, to working on my own. There are times when working for yourself can be lonely, there are few people to share your success with and no one to offload the stress onto when times get tough. Would I have it any other way? Absolutely not. Here I am today, the owner of a beauty business with a combined following of over 120,000 people, actively holding workshops around the country, teaching what I love, working as a make up artist for big name brands, styling the most amazing clothes, modelling, presenting, filming and editing videos, running a website and now writing my own book. I still pinch myself every day when I wake up with a beaming smile plastered across my face knowing this is all because I never gave up.

Chapter 2

Make Up
Magic

Product Positivity

What would a book by The Make Up Fairy be without a chapter on make up?! Having worked in the industry for the past eight years I've gained an extensive amount of experience and dealt with hundreds of faces.

From my experimental college years and on-counter retail days, to working on shoots, back stage on set and with a regular clientele of my own, I've collated a decent number of tips and tricks of the trade. I think the main thing I love about cosmetics, aside from the creative element, is their transformative ability. From smoky eyes that make you feel sultry and sexy to concealing cancer patient scarring, make up can bring bundles of confidence. I also love how feminine I feel after applying a fresh face.

I always remember my Mum using make up in a subtle manner; she has great skin so it was never used to hide away or camouflage her natural beauty, but instead to bring it out. I think make up can simply be part of a routine that makes getting ready complete and brings an air of effort to your polished look. For me, make up makes me feel like an entirely different person; I look older when I wear it, my eyes look more defined and dramatic, and my features more prominent. I have no issues being seen without make up and have never relied solely on application to feel beautiful, but I certainly don't feel as sexy sans product.

As a teenager I played around with different looks and browsed the Boots aisles frequently. I think my first experimentation was with liquid eyeliner from Rimmel, one I still love to this day. I loved how the dark rim around my lash line made my eyes stand out and appear more cat-like. I've had plenty of beauty bloopers too and owned an obscene amount of frosted lipsticks in my time, which had that really horrific smell of plastic. Back then, lip products didn't have the super fancy ingredients and sweet scents they do now, and instead resembled more of a crayon-like texture and taste. My collection began to grow at the same rate my pencil case did throughout Art College and I utilised make up as a means to explore my artistic talents. Soon, my skill set improved and I went from frosty faux pas to advanced artistry. Once I reached the stage of teaching my own make up course, I realised I had a real talent in this area and I enjoyed passing on my knowledge and instilling confidence in those who wanted to up-skill. Now, having held workshops and master classes around the country, I've noticed that the same questions are asked by girls time and again, so this chapter is here to answer them.

Perfecting Primers

Creating the perfect base is something every woman wants to know about. After all, if you get the foundations right, everything else will somewhat fall into place. Starting off with good skin is an added bonus, but not an essential.

I've worked on so many varying skin types over the years that I've learned that almost every ailment can be camouflaged or enhanced. If you're looking to prime perfectly, then your skincare needs to be on point, which we will discuss later on in Chapter 9. After finding the right products to treat and soothe your skin, the next step is finding a primer.

Primer is a step that so many people skip because they feel it's unnecessary. The truth is, we all experience difficulties of some sort that will prevent our foundation gliding on and lasting like a dream. For many Irish women, redness and broken capillaries are a huge issue. The opposing shade to red on the colour wheel is green, and as a result green-based primers can counteract and dull down any high colouring. Teenagers and oily skin sufferers alike require a mattifying primer that will reduce shine and sebum production. Dry and dehydrated skin types need more moisture, so a hydrating primer is brilliant. There are even primers out there for more obscure skin issues like excess sallow tones, where a lilac primer is used in the same manner as a green colour corrector for redness. The opposing shade works on reducing the yellow undertones. There are also some great peach tone primers out there to work on age spots and excess freckles.

In general, most primers will work on the specific skin concern, fill in fine lines, wrinkles and open pores, smooth the skin and blur blemishes, adding longevity to your look. Silicone is a common ingredient in most primers that acts like a Polyfilla for the face; in the same way that you would never paint a cracked wall, you should never apply foundation directly without using a primer to smooth out your skin. A primer will fill in the cracks, meaning the foundation or war paint will apply easily and evenly.

My TOP 5 PRIMERS

Smashbox Photo Finish Foundation Primer promises a soft focus finish and does everything you would want a primer to do. The range is so popular that they devised a terrific tube to suit every skin type, and having worked for the brand over the years, I can vouch for it's amazing quality.

Benefit The POREfessional is the best oil-free formula out there that will diminish large pores and unsightly blackheads. The silky textured liquid is easy to apply, feels comfortable on the skin and gives a long-lasting result.

Laura Mercier Foundation Primer – Radiance is a luxurious option that gives luminosity to the skin and is loved by celebrity artists worldwide. If you want a dewy glow and brilliant base then this is fantastic.

Maybelline Baby Skin Instant Pore Eraser is a brilliant budget buy that rivals its high-end competitors. Both non-comedogenic and fragrance-free, it's suitable for sensitive skin and has super cute girly packaging that packs a punch.

L'Oréal Infallible Mattifying Base is the closest dupe to Smashbox Photofinish that I've found. The silicone texture is identical, it regulates shine, perfects pores and is a brilliant base for most foundation textures.

Fabulous Foundations

Once you have your primer sorted the next step is foundation, which can be a tricky task for even the most proficient product junkie. Finding the perfect brand, shade, texture, and finish isn't easy and can take some stressful shopping around.

Similarly to primers, there are foundations out there to suit every skin type and tone. Coverage also plays a massive part; from sheer to full, things can get very confusing. Once you've addressed your skin type and requirements, my suggestion is to always ask for a make over or sample using the foundation you're interested in. This will give you an idea of how the product in question looks during the day, how it lasts throughout the night and will allow you to figure out your overall feelings on the product. There's nothing worse than hearing rave reviews about a brilliant base only to spend €38 on a bottle and want to bring it back because it doesn't suit you. If you want a really light finish that shows your skin, then BB and CC creams, tinted moisturisers and face and body lotions are ideal. These products work on enhancing your natural beauty and give a glow with slight coverage that shows your skin. Most

liquid foundations will give the next level of coverage from light, to medium and finally full. My favourite type of liquid foundation is a buildable finish that gives you the option of medium to full, taking you from day to night. Cream foundations tend to be heavier in texture and therefore give more immediate coverage and longevity and often suit more mature skin types. Compact foundations tend to be the most heavy and least hygienic, giving a thick layer of product that leaves very little skin showing, creating more of a mask. Finally, mineral make up, which is made in powder form for the most part, contains active ingredients like amino acids to work on surface exfoliation as your wear, which gives superficial coverage with the added benefit of long term skincare. Although they're an excellent choice for users with sensitive skin, they can be a little messy in terms of application, leading to a lot of fall out. Lots of people end up finding two foundations they love and mixing them together to create a unique finish. I used to love strong full coverage finish foundations when I was younger but now despise that caked look. Just like seasonal weather changes, your skin and foundation requirements change too. For example, in summer I love a breathable dewy finish that shows my skin but keeps me covered and confident at the same time, while during the cooler months I require more coverage.

My TOP 5 FOUNDATIONS

Yves Saint Laurent Le Teint Touche Éclat is my Holy Grail, dewy skin foundation. Everything from the luxurious packaging to the lightweight formulation is perfect. The buildable liquid coverage targets shadowy areas and highlights the contours of the face, making it a magic make over product that's definitely worth trying.

NARS Sheer Glow is marketed as a sheer foundation, but gives the most perfect amount of coverage. If you're looking for model-like skin, then this is a definite win. The bottle is sophisticated and dispenses the ideal amount of product and you only need a small amount, meaning a little goes a long way.

Mac Face and Body is an essential everyone should own, in fact I've yet to come across a Make Up Artist who doesn't keep at least one bottle in their kit. This lightweight lovely is designed to give the perfect 'your skin but better' look, can be buffed into bruises on the legs or applied for a fresh-faced look.

Inglot HD Perfect Cover Up Foundation is enriched with white truffle extract, which keeps the skin moisture-balanced. Suitable for sensitive skin, this medium to full coverage foundation is excellent for concealing blemishes and giving a medium to full flawless finish without looking caked.

L'Oréal True Match is the best budget buy base in my experience. Formulated with a fancy technology to adapt to your colouring and control your coverage, it contains no oils, fragrances, or pore-clogging fillers. A little goes a long way, it blends like a dream and glides on effortlessly.

Contouring

When it comes to contouring, there are so many ways to work wonders on shaping your face. Gone are the days when sparkly bronzer was applied all over to give a glittery glow, now the average individual can apply powders and cream products like a professional to create cheekbones, slim jawlines and even correct flawed features.

Ever since Kim Kardashian posted that popular picture with cream and brown stripes placed strategically all over her face, everyone has wanted in on her sculpting secrets. The concept is simple in theory; using products two shades lighter than your foundation to highlight certain areas and contouring with products two shades darker to add shadows. Unfortunately, most people find this method challenging and blending so many products can have you ending up looking like someone who dipped their head in a bowl full of Nutella. The most basic starting point to contouring is concealing. Starting off with a lighter shade makes the whole process easier to blend, and highlights the areas you want to stand out. Most people suffer with dark circles of some sort, so a liquid or cream concealer that will combine coverage with colour-correcting properties is ideal. Whether you opt for a liquid and wand combo, cream pot applied with the finger tips or a feathery pen, applying the product in a 'V' shape beneath the eye area will ensure it's bright and there's no overload of product that will in turn crease.

If you're going the whole hog in terms of contouring, then applying concealer to anywhere you want to protrude can be done at this point. For example the centre of the forehead, down the bridge of the nose, upwards at either side of the mouth and under the cheekbone hollows. This will give a natural guideline as to where your contour should be applied. In general, everyone wants strong cheekbones so applying a matte bronzer, powder or cream to this area is advised. If you want to slim the face, then adding the same contour to either side of the temple will naturally bring in the face by narrowing it out. If you're conscious of the width of your nose then applying contour with a smaller brush to either side will do the same trick. Finally, if a double chin is your concern, then sweeping some powder beneath the jawline and centre of the chin will make the fatty highlighted area recede. Whatever you decide to work on, be sure to use a matte product. Applying glitter or sparkly bronzers defeats the purpose of contouring as they contain particles that will highlight the face and undo your work. After priming the face, working in some foundation, and contouring, you can then see what areas need concealing. Finding a concealer that works well both under the eyes and on blemishes means minimising product use.

My TOP 5 CONTOUR PRODUCTS

Charlotte Tilbury Filmstar Bronze & Glow Compact is the perfect universal blend of pearl and pigment to contour features and mimic a sun-kissed complexion. The colour combo is travel friendly and flatters any skin tone, with colour-rich pigments that melt into the skin unlike any other powder product I've tried.

Nars Radiant Creamy Concealer has a luxurious texture and luminous finish, with a lightweight medium to high buildable coverage applied with a wand. The hydrating and light diffusing ingredients make it excellent for hiding imperfections and diminishing fine lines and dark circles.

Urban Decay Naked Skin gives the best buildable, even, semi-matte coverage I've ever come across. No matter how much you apply, it blends beautifully and doesn't crease or settle into crows feet. The flat wand is both innovative and ideal for the under eye area and the formulation works on unsightly break-outs too.

Mac Mineralise Skinfinish in **Give Me Sun** is the ultimate light golden glow, ideal for adding warmth to the face and contouring in a natural way. The formulation means it's easy to apply and one of my streak-free favourites.

L'Oréal Lumi Magique Touch Of Light Highligter helps to brighten the appearance of eyes and acts as a hydrating highlighter. It can be used to disguise tiredness and attract light on the cheekbones, brow bones and the Cupid's bow. A brilliant, budget buy for those trying out cream contouring for the first time.

Strobing

Strobing is a relatively new concept to the make up world. The art of contour has taken a back seat and in its place is a wonderful wave of new natural enhancement.

The technique focuses exclusively on highlighter, applied where light would naturally hit your face. Instead of requiring a contour to accentuate slimmer areas, applying soft shimmery shades to the right areas will naturally make the sections either side appear shaded. If you're a fan of glossy, dewy, radiant, fresh, and healthy skin then this is a skill you should learn.

In the context of contouring, highlighters are generally concealers or cream products used to disguise dark circles or blemishes and applied to make certain areas more pronounced. When it comes to strobing, highlighters can be creams, liquids or powders that contain iridescent particles that will reflect natural daylight, giving you a glow J-Lo would be jealous of. Unfortunately, like any new trend, people can take the technique too far. Instead of a subtle strobe they look decidedly sweaty, so it's important to be minimal with this type of make up. Choosing a moisturiser that adds a dewy look is a good place to start. Ensuring you use a highlighter that matches your skin tone is also important. If you have a sallow, olive complexion then you can get away with golden tones, if you have naturally fair skin, champagne and lemon highlighters tend to work best and the average medium skin colour will work well with warmer peach shades. The next stage is choosing where to highlight, so if you're familiar with contouring then the same highlighted areas apply. The highest point of the cheekbones, either side of the temples, down the bridge of your nose, below your brow bone, the inner corners of your eyes, and above your Cupid's bow should be the focal points. Be sure to blend the product in well to avoid looking greasy and if you have oily skin, follow up with a mattifying powder to set your silky look and opt for a powder blusher to add some colour.

My TOP 5 HIGHLIGHTERS

the Balm Mary-Lou Manizer is my Holy Grail, favourite highlighter of all time. This best-selling compact can be used to add extra definition to any area and the shade literally suits every skin tone. The powder is finely milled and super pigmented in just one sweep and ideal for the cheeks and collar bone, or as a wash of colour on the eyelids.

Mac Mineralise Skinfinish in Soft & Gentle is probably the most popular product around in terms of a universally suitable highlighter. Part of the Mineralise Skin Finish line, this luxurious powder has a velvety texture yet high frost finish. This is a must for any make up artist and lasts a lifetime.

Inglot Sparkling Dust is my luxury, loose, multi-use pick that gives the most gorgeous glow. This frosted fancy is highly pigmented and provides extreme pay off that's not chunky. One of the things I love about this product is how it can be applied in so many ways: on the skin, to the eyes, mixed with lip gloss, nail enamel, foundation, moisturiser, or a mixing medium to add a touch of sparkle to your look.

No7 Skin Illuminator Radiance Boosting Beauty Fluid is my liquid love. This radiance-boosting beauty has a brilliant brush for easy application and contains particles of iridescent shimmer that reflect the light in a subtle manner giving your skin a perfectly healthy glow.

Essence Soo Glow! is one of the best highlighters around if you're pinching pennies. The cream to powder formulation feels every inch high end and there are a couple of colour choices which work well applied with the fingertips or brush during the day or night.

Colour

When it comes to adding colour to your visage, things start to liven up a bit. Even after contouring or strobing, the face can look a little flat without blusher, so choosing the right product will really take your look to the next level.

From deep rose shades to the perfect pink or coral there's something out there for everyone. There are also a variety of textures to choose from, which range from pigmented powders to coveted cream finishes. If you have oily or combination skin I would recommend opting for a powder in terms of longevity. Depending on your base, powders will stand the test of time and not upset the products used underneath. Cream blushers give a gorgeous glow, but can sometimes remove your foundation, leaving you looking patchy instead of peachy. However, cream blushers applied to more mature skin or those who suffer with dry patches can bring a new level of life to an otherwise dull complexion. Meanwhile, multi-coloured blushers

are great for those who want to mix up their swish of colour depending on their mood. There are also some shimmer bricks out there that contain sparkling warm tones suitable for the cheeks, meaning you can skip the strobing and apply a two-in-one product. When blusher is applied correctly, it will jazz up the face in a natural way, enhancing the end result of your look. Unfortunately, so many people get the application part wrong and end up looking more Noddy than natural. The fullest part of the cheek, also known as the apple, is a general guide for colour, however it's a common mistake to bring your blusher upwards, sweeping it across the tip of their cheekbones. This gives a fake red highlight to an area that should be light not bright. Using your brush to scoop the apple of the cheek, working the product under the apple upwards gives a really complimentary look that's youthful and radiant.

My TOP 5 BLUSHERS

Charlotte Tilbury Cheek To Chic is my blow out blusher of choice. The innovative 'Swish & Pop' two-tone products have swoon-worthy status. Each shade has a creamy, colour rich texture containing finely crushed pearls to give your skin a limitless glow. My favourite is the perfect pink 'Love Glow'

Stila Convertible Colour is by far the best cream blush I've ever tried. A multi-use product, these compacts can be applied to the apples and or lips for a sheer or full on tint. Simply tap with two fingers and match your cheeks to you pout. 'Gerbera' is a great starter shade and 'Gladiola' is a fun orange that makes any tan pop.

Mac Powder Blush naturally has one of the widest ranges of textures and tones. Designed by, and for professionals, each compact is formulated to provide fantastic colour with ease and consistency. The choices are endless in terms of colours, but my go-to shades include 'Peaches' and 'Margin'.

NYX Powder Blush delivers high end results with super cute packaging and sheer, silky colour. The formula is highly pigmented, for a bargain buy, and the pay-off lasts all day. Available in 24 radiant colours, my picks include 'Ethereal' and 'Pinched'.

Bourjois Little Round Pot Blush has been around for almost 150 years and has made the brand famous worldwide thanks to its amazing texture and packaging. The baked, ultra-fine pressed powder smells like roses, shows up with one sweep and they even have a NARS Orgasm dupe called 'Rose D'Or'.

Brilliant Brows

Brows not only frame the face, they can also make you look more groomed and take years off your look. When I was a teenager, I attacked mine with a tweezers, meaning there's very little left near the ends.

As a result I've tried and tested every product out there to achieve a strong and defined yet natural look. I used to love using brow pencils to achieve a bold brow but find that they're a little on the harsh side. Most kohls coat the hair and skin giving a fake line as opposed to replicating natural follicle growth. Using a shadow that matches your brows, or a designated brow powder with an angled brush can give a really nice natural finish. The powder coats your hair and fluffs up any sparse areas meaning it's great for more mature women lacking in the hair department. Using a brow gel is also a really nice way to get a long-lasting look, give the appearance of hair and add definition with simple strokes. I personally love to use a gel to carve out the main arch and structure of my brow, feather the leftover product throughout and then finish with a lighter powder to look less harsh. This mixture of products creates the most defined natural look and sculpts your eyebrows to perfection.

My TOP 5 BROW PRODUCTS

Inglot AMC Eyebrow Gel When this became available on the Irish market, it fast became my favourite product. The waterproof pot is perfect for filling in the eyebrows, emphasising their colour and giving a distinct contour. The formula contains nourishing ceramides and lasts all day.

Mac Fluidline gel liners are available in 19 shades and are a brilliant, multi-use product. Meant for the eyes, they glide on effortlessly and last all day. The consistency is also perfect for the brows and the shade 'Dipdown' is the best warm brown I've tried and is ideal for redheads and brunettes alike.

Benefit Brow Zings is my compact of choice when it comes to natural, powder-filled brows. The cute case comes with a coloured wax and a soft powder to blend and fill in your brows, which is available in various shades to suit your hair colour, two brushes for application and even a tweezers to tame strays hair.

Soap & Glory Archery Brow Tint and Precision Pencil is an affordable multi-use option. The double-ended product has a pencil and pen to help you get your shape perfect. The stain and colour pay-off is excellent and lasts all day and it's a doddle to use.

Rimmel Professional Eyebrow Pencil is great if you want to stick to a pencil while saving some pennies. The pencil itself is creamy and pigmented and the shade range is decent. The lid has a flat brush that brushes through the brows and easily blurs away any harsh lines for a natural finish.

Subtle To Smoky

Artistry of the eyes is my favourite part of make up application. I love combining shadows, pigments and glitters to create unique looks. On days when I'm working in town or have some meetings, then simplistic subtle looks work nicely.

The great thing about shadows is how they can transform your look, completely taking it from day to night in an instant. Purchasing palettes that move from matte to shimmer and light to dark is travel friendly and far more convenient than single pot products. I rarely invest in individual items anymore and lean towards best-selling creations that have been released on the make up market.

There are no rules when it comes to eye work, but certain shades will enhance your natural colouring. If you have blue eyes, for example, then gold, yellow and orange tones will enhance them, really making them pop. If you have green or hazel eyes then heather, purple and

burgundy tones will make them stand out. If you have brown eyes you can pretty much get away with all shades, as they're dark enough to react to most contrasting colours. Pigmented shadows with little fallout are the easiest to work with if you're a newbie on the eye front, whereas loose pigments and glitters are a little more tricky. Using a gel-based mixing medium or fixing spray can help these products adhere to your skin better and help it to appear more vibrant. Similarly, an eye primer will work on reducing sebum production, increase pigmentation and aid the longevity of your shadows.

My TOP 5 EYESHADOW PALETTES

Urban Decay's Naked Palette series hold 12 eye shadow shades that run all the way from office appropriate neutrals, summertime bronzy looks to sultry smokiness. Each palette suits specific eye colours, the shadows are easy to apply with little to no fall out and even contain a travel-sized brush perfect for packing if you're taking a trip.

Lorac's Pro Palette was created by celebrity make up artist Carol Shaw and is favoured by beauty gurus and artists alike. Packed with 16 eye shadows (8 shimmer and 8 matte) it has every shade you could possibly need. The velvety shadows are highly pigmented and even infused with soothing botanicals.

the Balm NUDE 'tude Palette consists of 12 wearable shadows, each of which has a satiny smooth texture. The packaging is extremely cute and retro, making it stand out from rival brands. There's a lovely light highlighter all the way up to a bold burgundy taking you from day to night with ease.

The Pippa Palette was created by fellow blogger, friend and amazing entrepreneur Pippa O'Connor. This girly set is super for an overall natural look on the go. It's made up of 6 gorgeous nude-toned, matte finish, pigmented eyeshadows. It also has 3 face shades including a peachy pink blush, matte warm brown bronzer and shimmering highlighter.

The Sleek i-Divine Eyeshadow Palettes are the best budget buys I've come across in terms of shadow quality and colour range. Each set contains 12 brilliantly bright, super pigmented, long lasting, mineral-based eyeshadows. From nice neons to sexy smoky selections there are pearlescent particles for everyone.

Liner and Lashes

No eye look is complete without a lick of liner, lashings of mascara or a set of fluttering false lashes. Taking your cut crease or bold blended shadows to the next level, liner and lashes add delicate or daring drama.

In terms of liner there are three main categories, which include kohl, gel and liquid. Kohl pencils work best smudged into the upper waterline or applied to the lower waterline, closing in the eye and intensifying your look. Gel liners, my personal favourite, are the easiest to apply with a brush and work well on the upper and lower lid to create a thin or thick cat flick. Lots of gel liners can also be used through the brows, making them a multi-use product. Lastly, liquid liners give the most precise finish when applied correctly. The fine felt tip or thin brush bristles are designed to glide along the lashes for a glossy, bold finish. Mascara can add volume, length and curl to otherwise limp lashes. Whether you chose a subtle brown, bold black or bright shade, it's a must for any eye look. Choose from big bristles for lots of layering, rubber wands for instant oomph, or smaller combs for definition. If you're feeling extra flirty, then false lashes will really open up the eyes. There are individual and strip options and even semi-permanent application available in most salons now. Whether you want a cheeky curl added to your corners, or a full on fluffy effect, there are so many amazing ranges to choose from. Once you use the right glue, allow it get tacky and practise the perfect application, either with your fingers or tweezers, you're good to go.

My TOP 5 EYE PRODUCTS

Inglot Liners are by far my favourite. Their gel product pots are the most intense, pigmented shades I've ever tried, they're easy to apply and last forever. They dry in 30 seconds, are water, sweat and heat-proof and pretty much invincible. Be sure to use a decent, oil-based eye make up remover at the end of the night though. Their kohl liners are also excellent and stand the test of time on your waterline.

Yves Saint Laurent Volume Effet Faux Cils Mascara has been my Holy Grail lash lengthener for the past six years. This high end product, in all its golden glory, gives the ultimate false lash effect and even cares for your lashes. The nylon fibre brush coats each hair for maximum volume from root to tip, while B5 Pro Vitamin strengthens and protects.

L'Oréal Miss Manga Mascara is a relatively recent find that now features in almost all of my looks. The affordable formula contains enlarging collagen spheres which work in conjunction with the 360° flexible, cone-shaped brush to amplify upper lashes and reveal lower lashes.

Duo Eyelash Adhesive is the safest striplash glue and has been a favourite of professional makeup artists for decades. This latex-based formula can be worn all day even on the most sensitive eyes. Whether you choose to use this on individual or strip lashes you're guaranteed maximum hold with no nasty side effects.

Eylure Lashes in texture style No.117 are my most regularly purchased pack. They contain a long-angled style with a twisty, messed up finish for extra length and thickness and a set of corner lashes, which can be layered on top for added drama or worn alone for a more natural finish. They're easy to apply, feel like real hair and can be re-used up to three times.

Luscious Lips

There's nothing quite like completing your look with lashings of lip products. Probably my favourite kind of make up shopping, choosing a bright new bullet or lavish lip gloss makes me feel instantly made up and ready for my day.

I own hundreds of nude shades, revel in picking up the perfect pink, keep my coveted corals for holidays and brave a bold red or burgundy on the odd occasion. The selection of lip products out there is endless, from precision lip liners to define your look and ensure long-lasting wear to sheer shades that work on hydration.

Investing in at least one natural lip liner shade is essential. A warm rose to light brown tone will work with most nude, brown and pink lip shades. Depending on your preference, shopping for lipsticks should be a fun and experimental treat. There's no right or wrong when it comes to colours, however it's wise to select shades that will enhance certain features and colourings. A blue-toned red will make your pearly whites extra bright, while an orange undertone will enhance your tan. Most pink shades will bring out the yellow in your teeth, so be careful. Coral shades work best in the summer when the skin is more sallow but also complement red heads with freckles and fair skin really well year-round.

The ultimate nude can complete the smokiest of eyes in a demure way, and a brown with a purple undertone will channel your inner Kylie Jenner. Dark vampy shades like burgundy and wine work well with porcelain and olive skin tones and pair perfectly with simple liner and lash looks. The textures and finishes also change the overall look and feel of you lipstick. Descriptive words like satin, frost, glaze, matte, and cream are terms you should become familiar with. If your lips are dry then mattes will cause issues, so applying a hydrating lip balm prior to application will help the product stay on without highlighting cracked areas. Creamy textures work well on everyone and are a safe option if you're unsure. Finishing off your look with a lip gloss will also change the finish, giving it a shiny more voluminous look. If you're looking for an extra pucker plump then gloss can give you that 3D effect. Avoid sticky finishes where possible as they tend to look more gloopy than gorgeous and are a nightmare to keep on, not to mention when the wind blows through your hair.

My TOP 5 LIP PRODUCTS

EOS Lip Balm is a favourite of mine. EOS stands for evolution of smooth and will have your lips prepped for any product. Each beautiful ball coats both lips with natural conditioning oils, moisturising shea butter and antioxidant vitamins C & E to nourish. 'Coconut Milk', 'Pomegranate Raspberry' and 'Sweet Mint' are my go-to picks of this balm bunch.

Charlotte Tilbury Lip Cheat pencils are my all-time favourite lip liners. The shades 'Iconic Nude' and 'Pillow Talk' are investments every girl should make and they work with all neutral lip shades. The packaging is divine and the velvety, waterproof texture glides effortlessly giving a sexy shape to the lips that lasts.

MAC Lipsticks are at the perfect price point for purchasing high quality, on trend shades that are pigmented and long-wearing. The brand has the most diverse textures and unusual shades, meaning you'll always find exactly what you're looking for. 'Lady Danger', 'Ruby Woo', 'Rebel', and 'Snob' are some of my most-worn.

Rimmel's Lasting Finish Lipstick Collection by Kate Moss contains my budget buy bullets of choice. The affordable price point gives you premium packaging, pigmented pay-off of high intensity colour, great shade ranges and hydrating finishes. '01', '03' and '43' from the new nude collection are always in my make up bag.

Yves Saint Laurent Gloss Volupte is the most glam, light-weight, non-sticky lip gloss I've ever tried. The unique applicator envelops the lips perfectly while the centre hole dispenses just the right amount of product. The gloss smells gorgeous, the texture is like nothing I've ever tried before or since and the high shine finish is fabulous. There are 23 shades to choose from but '210' is my all-time favourite.

Brush Rush

No make up collection would be complete without some brilliant brushes to apply your make up. You can have the most coveted cosmetics collection going and without the right tools, application will be a difficult task.

So many of my clients have had trouble with blending eye shadow, for example, and it's simply been down to changing from a flat to a fluffy brush. Once you invest in the right kit your confidence will grow and you'll hopefully have your brushes for life once you look after them correctly. If you're only starting to build your collection, I would highly recommend purchasing brush sets as opposed to individual items. Most brands offer affordable options nowadays that contain the basic face and eye tools you need to get started. If you're a more experienced artist then certain brushes will naturally catch your eye and can be added to an already extensive collection.

A foundation brush, powder/bronzer, contour/brush, brow/eyeliner, flat shadow, fluffy shadow, definer and lip brush are the main bristles you need to achieve almost any look. I have hundreds of brushes at this stage in my career and I tend to stick to that selection for the most part. Different shapes and sizes will give different finishes. For example, a flat foundation brush will give the most coverage, whereas a duo fibre will give a more sheer, dewy, buffed-in look. Hygiene is hugely important when it comes to brushes so finding an easy way to wash and maintain them is essential. I would recommend using an alcohol based cleanser to quick clean your brushes between uses and a good clarifying shampoo for weekly cleansing, especially on the facial brushes as they carry most bacteria. Make sure to only wet the bristles as water will break the bonds and allow them air dry.

My TOP 5 BRUSH BUYS

Charlotte Tilbury brushes are the most beautiful brushes in the business if you can afford to splurge. Her complete set of eight essential brushes blend, smudge and buff flawless foundation, seductive smoky eyes, and perfect pouts. The sustainable wooden handles have also been cleverly angled so they won't roll off your table.

Real Techniques are by far my favourite brushes of all time. Created by the dynamic duo Pixiwoo they tick every box in terms of terrific tools. The beautiful packaging, great price point, shed-free brushes pick up product perfectly, they're super soft and the shapes are ideal for any artist.

Sigma Brushes are favoured by many a make up artist and beauty guru. The quality and functionality is fabulous and all of their products are handmade. I love this line for complete sets of brushes, ideal for extending your collection. They wash well, retain their shape and last a lifetime.

Blank Canvas is an award-winning, Irish cosmetics brand that create affordable and highly covetable makeup brushes and cosmetics. Lots of their brushes have become cult beauty favourites and their hot pink flat top foundation brush has been featured by bloggers everywhere.

Spectrum Brushes combine affordability with colourful collections unlike any other brand. The ombre brush sets are the ideal girly gift and the quality is superb. Both vegan and cruelty-free, they are magically manufactured to avoid shedding and pick up and apply product like a dream.

Cosmetic Conclusions

As you can see, there's a lot more to make up than meets the eye and building your beauty wardrobe can take time and money.

If you're struggling to put aside cash for aesthetic additions then jotting down a wish list is a great way to keep track of what you really want and perhaps ask for items when your birthday or Christmas comes around. If you have some money set aside to make a purchase of any of the above, browsing online beauty retailers is one of the handiest ways to shop. From the comfort of your own home you can browse bargains, check reviews, look up swatched shades and pop your decisions into a basket. One of the best online websites I've found that stocks most of the items I've mentioned above is Cloud 10 Beauty. I love supporting Irish business and this one-stop shop is making waves amongst make up junkies everywhere. Make up shopping and experimentation should be a positive experience, so finding the right retailer is also key if you don't like shopping online. Heading in to counters where you trust the staff and their skill set is also integral. Make up can lift your mood, make you feel prettier, enhance the features you were blessed with and switch up your look on the daily.

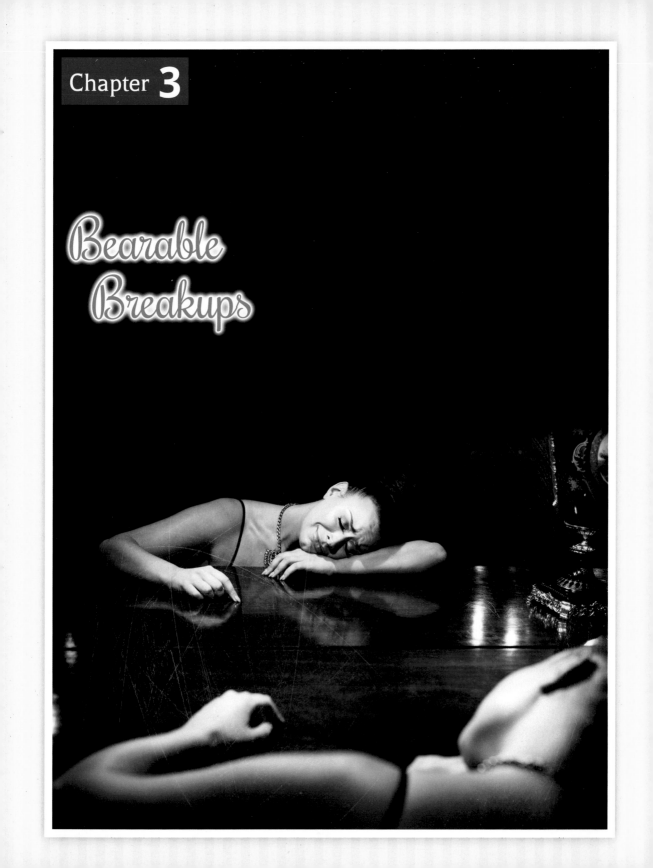

Chapter **3**

Bearable
Breakups

Never Settle

There's no denying that experiencing a break up can be one of life's toughest challenges. Healing a broken heart can take months, even years, and it's one of the most mentally draining experiences we all endure at some point.

There's no better feeling than that honeymoon phase; sharing your life with someone special, those good morning texts, having someone to talk to at the end of a rough day, cuddly movie nights and knowing you've a caring plus one at special occasions. Many people marry their first love, some stay single for the majority of their adult life, while others trial and test various partners in a bid to find the perfect one. If like me you're in the latter category, you refuse to settle for anything less than fireworks and are willing to patiently work towards finding your soul mate. Unfortunately, falling into this category means you'll likely experience plenty of frustration, mind games, tears and sorrow, with honeymoon phases few and far between. I've been through my fair share of break ups throughout my 28 years on this earth. I love being in love and spent my youth in and out of long-term relationships. I guess, when I was younger, I was scared of being alone and became accustomed to being someone's other half, and I struggled just being me. A terrible mindset to have, I was naive and didn't find myself or realise what it was like to truly be alone and grow until my mid twenties.

My First Boyfriend

At the age of 14 I had my first real relationship. He was five years my senior and my poor parents were less than happy with my first choice of other half.

I honestly don't know how my poor mother didn't have a heart attack when I brought him home, expecting everyone to accept the situation. A typical teenager, I was rebellious and wild with a 'know it all' attitude. The group I socialised with was a mixture of girls my own age and older guys, so that sort of age gap in relationships became normalised. He was my friend's older brother and at the time I'd had a crush on him for a while, so jumped at the chance of being his girl. During my alternative phase we were the perfect pair; he was a tall rocker in a band, had long blonde dreadlocks and piercings and I felt small and very cool beside him. A fairy far removed from the one you know now, I had various bright colours throughout my hair and wore ripped jeans and slashed tops accompanied by severely over-plucked brows.

A typical teenager, I was rebellious and wild with a 'know it all' attitude.

He was somewhat of a leader in the group and we hung out, for the most part, in the cul de sac of his road and listened to music outside playing from his bedroom window. In fairness, he was a caring boyfriend; he treated me well and we had some fun times but the age gap, as could be expected, caused issues. He had zero ambition (you'll notice a pattern as I continue my story), he worked in a supermarket and played guitar at weekend gigs. I was sitting my Junior Cert at the time and struggling to focus on exams. The relationship ended after a rather dramatic argument about the fact that I felt he was lazy and never ready when I called over. It consisted of some shouting and me spilling water over his guitar as we both agreed we had no future together. He went on to go out with someone twice my age and I moved on relatively quickly too, gradually washing that man, and colour, right out of my hair.

Growing Up

Fast forward four years and I had kissed a few frogs and thankfully grown out of my alternative appearance and skinny eyebrows into a glamorous girly girl.

I had moved on and waved goodbye to that circle of acquaintances and gained lots of new-found friends, some of whom became best pals for life. I had a horse during this stage and spent a huge amount of time at the yard I stabled him, in hanging out with fellow horse lovers and almost regaining my lost innocence and childhood. At my 18th birthday party I had my pick of two good guys. One was a little bit older, brought a bottle of wine as a gift for my parents and treated me like a princess. The other was a slightly younger stable boy who I ended up casually dating for about six months. I still look back at that time as my favourite age. I was happy in myself, had a great group of people around me, liked how I looked, spent my summers at festivals, dancing at concerts and going to clubs. I briefly dated a footballer for a while but culled it quickly when he told me he loved me after two weeks. I was in no rush to have a boyfriend again and enjoyed spending time with the girls. I visited my mum in London where she was living and acting in the West End. I was never short of male attention and had my pick of good-looking guys, there was no pressure to meet anyone and I just enjoyed and embraced everything.

First Love

Around the time of my Debs the good guy, the stable boy and a few new admirers were still on the scene. I wanted to pick a date that I didn't fancy or have any obligation to entertain so I took a friend who ended up trying to kiss me at the end of the night.

Shortly after this, on a night out, I was on the hunt for fresh meat and spotted someone I was instantly drawn to. With a head full of shocking black hair, beautiful bone structure, snow white skin, big brown eyes and the most gorgeous set of teeth and smile I had ever seen, he made something happen to my insides. As cliché as it sounds, you really can tell when someone is going to turn into something special. I gravitated towards him and, with a little Dutch courage, he became the first and last guy I ever came on to. I confidently asked him for a lighter for my friend, which I didn't need, and we began chatting. I was genuinely mesmerised by his features and couldn't tell you what we discussed, but I know it was something to do with looking for a job in the gym he worked in and I casually gave him my number in case anything cropped up. He asked me inside for a drink and while I went to the toilet to freshen up, he texted me while I was there saying 'PS. You're hot', which I thought was beyond smooth. We kissed in the rain that night and he put me in a taxi, and what began was what I like to call my real life version of *The Notebook* movie. My first real love, we spent every waking moment together thereafter for about two years. He took me on a trip to Paris after three weeks of knowing him and we loved each other to the point it hurt. We had horrifically intense arguments, amazing sex and the whole thing became addictive. My parents loved him and we spoke about marriage, I suppose I thought he was my soul mate.

My First Heartache

After a time he became ill and it put a huge strain on our relationship. We were both going through exams in college and barely saw each other.

Phone calls became strained and conversations changed. I knew it was coming and the day we ended our relationship was possibly one of the worst days of my life. Both in floods of tears, we knew what we shared had become unhealthy and had to end. I felt my whole world crash around me, I couldn't accept or hear the words coming out of his mouth. I had stupidly dropped friends and paused my life to love this person with every inch of my mind and body and when he removed himself I had nothing left. I spent a year rebuilding my life, regaining friends I had shunned to spend time with him and becoming strong again. I can honestly tell you I cried every single day and night for at least a year. I never thought I was going to be okay again or genuinely heal.

We bumped into each other on nights out and ended up going home together on numerous occasions, only to wake up empty and injured, unable to lick each other's wounds. We went back and forth so many times and every time drink was involved. He would call and hound me, telling me I was the one that got away and that he loved me more than life itself. Once he sobered up again he would distance himself, become cold and push me away, saying it was a mistake and we would never work. I ended up flying to Boston to stay with friends for two months that summer because I literally had to be away from everything to do with him. He continued to email me, once again getting into my head, making sure I didn't get over him and we met up when I returned to Ireland and I was back to square one. I eventually had to do everything in my power to ignore his contact from then on and start actually moving on.

I ended up flying to Boston to stay with friends for two months that summer because I literally had to be away from everything to do with him.

The first person I kissed after him was vile, I didn't want another man near me, nothing felt the same. Everything and everyone was boring. Until, one day, I woke up and the pain wasn't so bad anymore, it was like weaning myself off drugs, it gradually got easier. Up until two years ago I heard from this person on and off. Some years it was once or twice, others more frequently. We always reminisced on the good times, questioned if we had met at a later date would we have worked, asked ourselves would we ever find that kind of chemistry and love again. We even hooked up from time to time years on, essentially having an on and off relationship spanning seven years. He told me he would never love anyone the way he loved me, that he didn't want to and that was enough for me.

Long Term Love

During those seven years I met the person who became my longest relationship to date. After the heartbreak I felt as a result of my first love, I was loath to ever give myself to another person in that manner again.

In retrospect, I realise that at the time I needed to regain control and meet someone who would love me without as much risk of loss involved. I had met a guy in college before my *Notebook* love, who I had briefly flirted with. He had a girlfriend and we clicked on a friendship level with a base of attraction. During that mid-term break while I was asking my first love for a lighter, not knowing it was the start of something big, my college guy broke up with said girlfriend in a bid to confess his feelings for me. When we returned to college, he expressed his love for me and explained how he had ended things with his girlfriend and wanted to give things with us a go. I then had to explain that I was going to Paris with a guy I'd met in a smoking area a few weeks prior. Feast or famine.

I didn't speak to college guy for the two years I was in that relationship with my first love, but as fate would have it he got in touch with me when I was single post-Boston trip. He asked me how I had been, what I was up to and if I'd like to attend a fashion show he was DJ-ing at. I did. I was somewhat vulnerable and broken and closed off to love when we met up this time. We started seeing each other casually but I felt it had no future. He had turned into a bit of a bad boy, partied a lot, had a lot of female attention, was too promiscuous for my liking and didn't treat me very well. After a few months, he told me I deserved better and that he would be back when he was a prince and not a frog. As silly as that sounds, college guy actually went away, worked on himself and called me up about six months later to say he had changed and was ready for a relationship.

Breaking the Bad Boy

Our relationship had a rocky start. While I was away on holidays with my mum, he cheated on me but I didn't find out for about four months at which point we had progressed to an amazing place in our relationship.

I woke up one morning after a horrific nightmare that he had slept with someone at a party while I was abroad. When I explained the dramatic dream, the colour literally washed from his face. I asked if there was any truth to my gut instinct when I saw his ghostly reaction and he just crumbled, saying he didn't know how or when to tell me, that he had made a massive mistake and that it would be his last. He explained how the whole cheating experience had made him

realise that he genuinely wanted to commit to me more than ever and finally wave goodbye to his bad boy ways. We had come so far and he was such a good boyfriend to me at this point that I didn't know what to do.

I think the argument consisted of me slapping him across the face, asking him to leave, sobbing my heart out and him incessantly texting me romantic words. He came over that night with a book, ironically about fairy tales, and wrote his own apologetic story on the inside explaining how he was the gremlin playing in a garden filled with dark creatures until he found a beautiful fairy who changed his ways. I was so smitten by his seemingly heartfelt confessions and explanation that we decided to move on. College boy ended up being my committed boyfriend for four years. We went on holidays together, we rented an apartment, moved into a three-bedroom house and even bought two dogs.

Feeling Restless

Our families became close and assumed we would marry, but after time cracks started to show. I became unsettled and wanted more. I worried I was too young for such commitment and remember the exact moment of panic that changed everything.

Bringing the bins out and taking the dogs in while he was at work, I looked at the life I had created. It was essentially everything I thought I wanted. I was working as a teacher, had a beautiful home, a loving partner and two furry friends, but something was missing. I wanted more from life, I wanted a more successful and varied career path, I wanted to test out complete independence, I wanted to travel, I wanted to meet new people and experience new things. I felt claustrophobic and trapped. I didn't want to hurt anyone, I just wanted to leave quickly one day without anyone noticing. Having experienced true heart break I was loath to inflict it on someone who cared about me so much. Instead of expressing my fears and articulating my worry to my partner I started to detach, I grew cold and began going out clubbing and working all the time. I started my blog as a means to accrue new make up clients but also to start working towards my own life. I was always working, when he came home and wanted affection and attention I would go upstairs to be on the laptop. When he wanted to cook dinner together I preferred spending time with the girls. I became the most horrific girlfriend, I was falling out of love at a rapid pace and began resenting him for my situation.

Instead of expressing my fears and articulating my worry to my partner I started to detach, I grew cold and began going out clubbing and working all the time.

The Weak Way Out

On a night out with friends I met a guy who I instantly knew was bad news. I was intensely drawn to him and intrigued by his quirky personality.

I firmly believe that you know when there is an opportunity to potentially cheat, in which case you should walk away immediately and either address your issues or end your relationship. I clicked with this person on another level; we had very similar family issues and were both craving something new and exciting. That weekend, after a fight with my partner, I went out with a group of friends that included bold boy. We got very drunk and spent the entire night in the beer garden talking. Everything he said was music to my ears and I started to feel alive again. The missing spark and fire was in my belly and although the situation was wrong it felt so right. The next thing I knew we were kissing passionately and after a few moments I stopped, sobering up to the realisation of what I'd done. Everything had been leading to this point yet I hadn't stopped it. That night I stayed in a friend's house instead of going home and asked advice on how to handle the situation.

Would I tell the truth and break my partner's heart or forget it ever happened and move on? I decided to go home the following day, face the music and confess everything. Watching my long-term partner cry and hit the wall with anger was one of the hardest things to see. What was seemingly such a flippant move had turned an innocent party's world upside down. I remember him asking me how a silly kiss compared to a loving home where we decorated the walls and raised our dogs. I snapped back that he had cheated on me early on in the relationship but knew it wasn't comparable. I had no answers, I just wanted the relationship to end and for him to break up with me so that I didn't have to be the one to end things. I moved out for about two weeks and we spoke briefly about the house and looking after the dogs; general domestic discussions. At the end of our break he called me and said we needed to talk. Instead of ending things like I assumed he would and felt he should, he apologised, claiming the cheating was his fault, that something was obviously lacking for me to have to wander and that he wanted to address our issues and fix it.

Instead of jumping for joy at his forgiveness I felt impending dread. I was back to square one and couldn't turn down his kind gesture, surely I owed our relationship one last shot? Not surprisingly, it failed miserably, we fought constantly, bickered about bills and he became more controlling than ever. We were miserable, the trust was totally lost and everything reminded him of my mistake. Eventually we separated and moved out of the house, leaving with one dog each.

The Rebound Relationship

I don't think I cried once during our break up. As heartless as it sounds, I was so relived to be out of it, not because he was a bad guy, but simply because it wasn't working,

I had thought about getting out for so long and I hated the girlfriend I had become. Physically packing up my belongings into boxes was done on autopilot. I was briefly in touch with bold boy near the end of everything and we began pulling towards each other as soon as I was single. Instead of staying single and working on myself I jumped right into another relationship. Bold boy was the opposite of my ex in every way possible. He didn't have a jealous bone in his body, loved partying, wasn't in a stable situation whatsoever, didn't want anything serious initially but taught me how to have fun again. We went out A LOT, and lived a lavish lifestyle with champagne-filled parties, fancy meals, and shopping trips. We skipped happily through town late at night, kissing at corners and planning adventures. We became a fiery tag team, fuelled by similar interests and combined ambitions and all of a sudden it was six months in.

Bold boy was spontaneous at the best of times and completely unreliable at the worst. He started to want other things, I questioned his motives and my own. I wondered what I was doing with my life and how I had ended up in a relationship by accident. I was addicted to the adrenaline I felt when I was around him but felt guilt when I left him. I was guilty about my ex, guilty about my lifestyle and my lack of concrete plans. I was essentially living in a bubble that was about to burst. I needed to be on my own and learn to love myself before I could truly love anyone else again. I wanted to be selfish, I wanted to flourish and I wanted to deal with my demons. I had been in love or broken up with for the majority of my youth and I just wanted to find myself.

Learning to Be Alone

I spent the next two years being single for the most part. Bar a few smooches and texting tales along the way I was just Joanne.

I spent time on my own, focused on my career, worked long hours and immersed myself in The Make Up Fairy. I regularly went out with the girls and thrived on my jam-packed schedule. I met

a few dodgy characters along the way that put me off ever dating again. At the end of the two years I started to miss having someone. I had adequately worked on myself, I had an amazing career, a great group of friends, and a fantastic family but I wanted to fill the final void.

For me, a huge aspect of dating is the excitement and affection. Human contact is so important and if you're a girl who's not promiscuous then that only occurs when you're in a relationship. I was never a fan of one-night stands and took sex seriously, so I had to really connect with someone before giving anyone a part of me. I went on holidays to Spain, Punta Cana and Marbella that year and it's safe to say I had fun. I had a few holiday romances and began casually dating when I returned home. Although I had a few boyfriends I had never properly dated, I had always met guys naturally through friends and sort of fell into relationships.

At this point, dating apps were quite prolific and most of my friends were using Tinder to meet men. Long gone were the days when you could simply spark conversation by asking for a lighter, now you had to swipe left or right on your phone to go out for dinner. The whole thing made me nervous; meeting a stranger online in a bid to find love? With possibilities of being cat-fished, meeting a creep, or someone not looking like their profile picture, there were so many things that could go wrong.

Long Distance Dating

And let me tell you so many things did go wrong. I met pig after pig, each of whom only seemed to want me for my looks. They were either painstakingly arrogant with inflated egos or mind-numbingly boring.

I persevered and eventually matched with someone worth mentioning. Last year, I was showing my friend how to use Tinder when the most divine creature popped up. My type from head to toe, he was exotic standing at 6'4' with black hair, dark skin, brown eyes and amazing style. We began chatting and it turned out he was from London and through a glitch in the app we somehow came up on each other's feed. To be frank, he seemed too good to be true. Beyond hot, nice, funny, a male model and well-known photographer, meaning we also shared so many similarities by virtue of our industry. We chatted on Skype and sent texts every day for about two weeks. I then got impatient and decided the whole situation was silly because we lived in different countries and it would never work. In the lead up to my birthday, he called me and said he had a surprise. He had booked tickets to fly over to meet me on my birthday.

I literally couldn't breathe with excitement, I couldn't eat or sleep and I listened to dance music on repeat to try to expend my nervous energy. The day I collected him from the airport I was shaking, but the second I saw him I was relaxed. A true gent, we had the best night and kept in touch for a few months after he flew home. The distance became an issue and the casual nature of the relationship meant it was too expensive to maintain. Beautiful boy still texts me every now and then with a standard 'Hey you.'

Keeping the Faith

Instead of losing hope I continued to be an eternal optimist, treating every encounter as an experience when it came to love, and in September of last year I met someone I thought was the one.

He was my type looks-wise and the personality he portrayed was perfect. On paper his situation was far from ideal. He had just moved home from years living and working in Australia, he was well travelled but had no set career. An aspiring actor and model he was creative but lacked ambition and drive. There's a quote in one of my favourite movies, *Eat Pray Love*, that goes, '*I have a history of making decisions very quickly about men. I have always fallen in love fast and without measuring risks. I have a tendency not only to see the best in everyone, but to assume that everyone*

is emotionally capable of reaching his highest potential. I have fallen in love more times than I care to count with the highest potential of a man, rather than with the man himself, and I have hung on to the relationship for a long time (sometimes far too long) waiting for the man to ascend to his own greatness. Many times in romance I have been a victim of my own optimism.'

This sums up everything my relationship embodied. I was at the height of my career, I was booking jobs daily and holding my own workshops around the country and to be honest I had far more to bring to the table than he did. He began as a kind caring sort, he told me everything I wanted to hear. I felt lucky and safe in his arms and he was different to anyone I had been with before. He was immediately serious about us, there was no waiting around for a text or the next date. He introduced me to his family within two weeks, asked me to be his girlfriend after three and told me he loved me within a month.

> *He began as a kind caring sort, he told me everything I wanted to hear.*

Moving Too Fast

I was so happy but completely blinkered to the issues that were about to arise. He began to feel threatened by my success and started to question his own situation. He decided of his own accord to leave his job and move to Dublin.

He rushed and pushed our connection, almost as if to answer his own life questions. He didn't know where he was at, he spoke of missing Oz and moving back there, but then the following day would excitedly speak of getting a mortgage here with me. I was pushed and pulled throughout every inch of his indecision and I went along with it because I genuinely believed he was worth it. I assured myself that nothing was ever perfect and I would end up a crazy cat lady if I kept trying to find it. I was constantly worried and stressed. From the outside we seemed the perfect pair from but behind the scenes I was working constantly to please him. His energy was so low at times that I became fragile and the independent, strong woman I fought so hard to be was slowly being shattered. Instead of making me feel loved through his actions, he instilled insecurity by emotionally tormenting me. He was tight with money, another essential ingredient that was missing and I overlooked.

I'm a generous person by nature and he made me feel guilty for wanting to do and give nice things. He made me second guess every positive trait I had. One morning I woke on one of the many hotel stays I received as a perk of my job and he asked me why I could never get ready and shower before him instead of just being there like a heavy pressure waiting for hugs. My heart broke in two at how cold and cutting he could be, but I still stayed.

Feeling the Pressure

In hindsight, I was paranoid about being 27 and having to start all over again if we ended. He was also the first boyfriend I ever shared on social media, which at the time he loved and I was terrified about how I would explain things to my audience if things went tits up.

Things were up and down, and while we were on holidays he barely spoke to me or touched me until the point I begged him to explain what was going on. He said he felt he needed to return to Australia and figure himself out. He felt he was living in my shadow and rushed into the relationship with the hope that loving me would make him stay and be enough. The truth is that I was never enough and I walked away from that situation pretty hurt but thankfully not worse off. I had so much to give to someone who actually deserved it. I was self-sufficient, I cooked, cleaned, sent him to football matches, dressed up and integrated into his family and friends so well and yet I still wasn't adequate. I loved him with all I had but I wasn't smothering, I did my own thing and went along with his fast-paced suggestions but never pushed anything forward. I was a broken woman when that relationship ended. I wanted to delete every social media account and just hide under the duvet. I cried constantly over the time I wasted with him, wondering at how someone could seemingly wake up one day and stop loving you. The issue wasn't with him though, I allowed it all to happen and I was blinkered by the romantic ideals and physical attraction.

I ignored the warning signs and chose to continually see him as a good person. A close male friend asked me two questions when the relationship ended. Would I have dated said individual if I saw on paper his negative traits and lack of career, and would I be sad or relieved in five years time that we had ended? Suddenly everything wasn't so bad, and instead of dwelling on the pain like I had all those years before in my first real relationship, I immersed myself in a new challenge. The gym was such an amazing outlet for me during such a horrible time, the benefits went beyond my mind frame, the body changes meant I felt more confident and empowered than ever and said ex would be very sorry.

Learning From Love

As you can see by my relationship history it hasn't been easy, but it's been worth it. I'm not even 30 and I've lived and loved through some of life's most incredible and horrific moments.

I've inflicted and experienced every sort of heart break from young love to first love, lived with someone and raised pets, seen both sides of cheating and been on the rebound, been single, dated and woken up next to someone who wasn't in love with me anymore. After my cold-hearted ex, I stopped constantly going for my set type looks-wise and opened myself up to more important traits. Instead of going for the tall, dark and handsome guy who had nothing going for him I had a very specific checklist of characteristics and life circumstances that appealed to me in a man, after years of relationships with people who lacked those traits. I briefly dated a guy with a brilliant job, who was highly intelligent, ambitious and hard-working, he was settled, and most importantly kind, funny, caring and generous. He entered my life when I least expected it and I almost didn't go on our first date because I didn't think I would fancy him. I'm so thankful I did because he was proof that going outside your comfort zone shows you new experiences. However, that relationship also taught me to seek balance because dating a workaholic leaves very little time for being together in the present or planning the future.

Right now I'm happier than I've ever been in my life. I've found balance and I'm ready for someone who is on the same wavelength as me with regard to career and life goals. After everything I've experienced, though, I'm under no illusion that things will be perfect. The day I meet someone who fits into my life we will reach various bumps in the road, fight and maybe even break up. Nothing is guaranteed in this life and we simply have to keep our standards high and expectations low to survive. You could be happy in a partnership for ten years and one day it can stop working. Similarly you can be single and stressed and one day Mr. Perfect will walk in. You need to be open to love and heartache in equal measures. Keep your friends, talk to your family, and listen to their judgments on someone new. Keep your wits about you when a man feeds you with bullshit, make sure you're both on the same page. Ensure you express yourself at all times and if something isn't working learn to walk away. It's called a break up because it's broken; sure people can make mistakes and a leopard can somewhat change his spots but in general if someone is able to lose you, in their eyes you're not worth finding again.

Chapter **4**

Surviving
Singleton

Want Not Need

Whether you choose to be single or require time to come to terms with your new relationship status, this chapter is here to help you with heartache and celebrate being a strong, independent woman.

Although I'm speaking to you through these pages without knowing the turmoil you may be experiencing, I can hand on heart promise you it will be okay. Maybe not today, maybe not in a month, but day by day it will get easier until the magic moment you forget that it was ever hard. Countless times I've cried over a guy and firmly believed I would always feel that way, I've wasted emotions on men who I would walk by in the street now and barely feel the need to say hello to. As sad as it sounds, life moves on, people grow apart and the person you once shared every intimate detail with becomes a stranger.

I've also been single by choice but reached that stage of wanting someone in my life and worrying if I would ever find them. I've questioned if I would I be alone forever, lost faith in dating and the male species in general. Over the past year, however, I've really learned to love myself, so much so that anyone who enters my life is a bonus and not a requirement. I'm so busy being a boss lady that I've stopped worrying and wondering and started really living and loving. There's something so appealing about a girl who requires nothing from a man. I firmly believe that you have to really want to be with someone and not need to be with them in order for things to work out. When you focus your time and energy on working on yourself and for yourself, amazing things happen. Instead of coming across as needy on a night out or requiring a man to validate your existence, you're indifferent and if and when they come along, they're an awesome addition to your already fabulously full life.

Let People In

Over the past year or so my inbox has been inundated with emails and private messages from young girls and older women alike expressing how they've experienced heartbreak of some kind, asking how I've coped in the past and if I can offer any advice.

Learning to function and live your life without that special someone, when a split is fresh, can be a testing time to say the least. The generic advice of 'he's not worth your tears' or 'there are plenty more fish in the sea' simply doesn't cut it and can often irritate. Your personal circumstances and past experiences play a huge role in your road to recovery. If your family didn't support the relationship in the first place or you've lost some friends through it, the situation can be exacerbated because you feel there's no one to turn to. People around you can think 'I told you so' and as a result are reluctant to help. Perhaps they hated your ex from the start or warned you not to get back with him for the eighth time. Hopefully you have a core group of gal pals or at least one close friend who understands what it's like to go through a break up, someone who won't tire of your constant reversions and break up woes.

Family can also be fantastic, I know my mum is my rock when it comes to any sort of sad situation and she continues to listen, guide and support every decision I make, even when she knows from the start that I could do better or choose differently. She also tells me straight how it is instead of appeasing me and simply saying what I want to hear. Honesty is key from the circle of people who surround you because its those who are outside a situation who can often see something coming from a mile off and lack the emotion you've invested which can often make you blind to the truth.

Pushing Through the Pits

Losing love can be a lonely time, trust me I've been there. I've woken up after the initial break up disoriented and with a heavy heart.

That feeling of not wanting to lift your head from the pillow for fear the pain in your heart will knock you back down again is so familiar to me. I've had that sick feeling in the pit of my stomach where I know things have taken a turn for the worse and can't be mended. I've genuinely believed my life is over or not worth living without that special someone. I've wondered what they're doing at every moment of my day and cried until there were no tears left. I've stopped eating, sleeping and functioning. I've eaten ice cream and sobbed at the scene in *Sex & The City* where Big lets Carrie down on her wedding day. I've avoided going to parties for fear I would break down in a nightclub, or that I would see happy couples everywhere. I've driven past hotels my ex and I stayed in and felt as if I was being stabbed by the memories. I've stopped listening

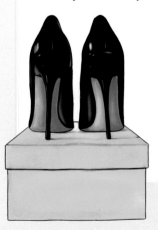

to music to avoid hearing every song that was 'our song'. I've written lists of why the person is no good for me yet ignored my own handwriting. I've given second chances when they weren't deserved and I've fallen in love with the idea of someone only to be surprised at the end outcome. I've had sleepless nights, I've obsessed over their Facebook page and panicked over the new girl commenting and I've generally lost the plot. The pain is indescribable and unless you've endured the devastation first hand, often hard to comprehend.

Women Are From Venus

So, how do you cope? Is it possible to move on? Will you truly be okay? Will you meet someone else? Well, before I address the former, the first piece of advice I can give you is to breathe.

This is the worst of it; the open wound needs time to heal and time really is the only thing that will plaster over that pain. The final argument and the words exchanged will play on your mind for at least a couple of weeks. You'll think of things you wish you had expressed, or said differently. You may only remember the good things about your ex and your mind will begin playing tricks on you, in turn persuading you to want him back. The first difficulty you'll undoubtedly face is not being able to contact him. Throughout a relationship, your partner in crime is there to share every moment of your day with, from calling them up just to simply say hi to calling over to cheer them up after a bad day. If a relationship has

ended, the worst thing you can do is maintain contact if feelings remain. If you call your ex, guess what? They probably have nothing new to say and repeating the fact that you're not working as a couple is probably going to hurt you even more to hear over and over again, like adding salt to a graze.

To be frank and blunt, if they aren't calling you they simply don't want to talk to you. Women analyse EVERYTHING. We create scenarios in our heads that don't exist and then have conversations with a partner who's probably thinking about what they'll have for breakfast while you sob into your pillow. Men are simple creatures who carry less emotion and handle things differently. When a man decides he no longer wants in on a relationship, he's thought long and hard about this decision for some time and will stick to it. They're pragmatic creatures, they feel a sense of freedom when they end things, while we mourn. Then, a few months later while we're over the entire fiasco and have moved on, they can often regress and realise they let something good slip through their fingers, all too little too late.

Day By Day

So, how do you stop contacting someone who was such a large chunk of your day? A huge part of this process is about changing your routine to avoid constantly having the desire to call, wonder what he's doing, what he's thinking about, why isn't he calling, or if there's someone else.

The main focus here should be you, what your day now consists of and how you can become happier and more fulfilled than ever. Wasting your time thinking about him and where he's at literally pauses your life and prevents growth. A break up should be dealt with like a learning process, sure it sucks beyond belief but there is a very obvious reason why it didn't work or wasn't meant to be, you just can't see it yet. The first task I suggest you work on is making a list of all the reasons why you're broken up and factually what wasn't working. Try to be as honest as possible; no one has to see this list, the words are there for your eyes only. The list can begin with small traits that annoyed you like the fact that John always left the toilet seat up or left his clothes lying around and eventually graduate to bigger issues like John was abusive and untrustworthy or a cold-hearted pig.

Sometimes pain can bring about so many emotions that we forget the concrete facts. We feel so much love for the person we've lost that we forget the fact that they treated us badly and ultimately weren't a suitable match. The sooner you realise he wasn't for you, the easier it is to accept, and acceptance is an ideal starting point for the grieving process. Grieving sounds dramatic and is usually associated with a death, but a break up can often feel like a death by virtue of the fact that the person is no longer with you in the same capacity and going through the motions is effectively grieving. Give yourself time to grieve.

Be Mindful of Memories

You'll have plenty of memories of your time together and regardless of the above list they will naturally surface, regularly bringing you back to the missing him stage.

My main advice here is to try to avoid idealising your past and reverting to the honeymoon phase in your memories. That time was wonderful and filled with joy but it's not a realistic comparison to your current situation and you're not losing the person you knew back then. Unfortunately, the dynamic must have changed dramatically in order for the relationship to have ceased and the more recent memories are the ones you should think about. Once you're aware of the facts of why it's not worth fighting for, then simply allow those fond and not

so fond feelings to pass through your mind, but don't dwell on them. One technique that really worked for me during particularly tough initial phases was a form of healing called Mindfulness. If you're having a particularly sad, sleepless night, for example, try the following activity. Try to vividly imagine your ex and the happy moments you shared together, then focus on the mental image, turning it black and white and letting the image get smaller and smaller until it becomes a dot you allow to float away from your mind. The opposite is then suggested for more recent negative memories, situations where you felt upset, angry or insecure.

Clearly see that time in your mind, that massive argument, allow the colours become vibrant, feel the anger you felt, make the picture bigger and more highlighted in your mind. Focus on every emotion and every detail and repeat the process. This may sound like a hippy dippy method but I can tell you first hand it works. The exercises focus on your breathing and concentration and help you to store memories in the correct head space without the blinkered emotion you're experiencing at the time. When you're extremely upset, your judgement can become clouded and files can go into the wrong 'feelings folders' as I like to call them.

Online Upset

The next big challenge so many people face after a break up or during difficult times is dealing with social media. It is a part of our every day lives.

And after a break up it often means that we have to see everything our ex is doing online and update our relationship status for the world to see. Social media puts a huge pressure on people to save face, live a luxurious life and portray the image of a perfect couple. In actuality, things are far more boring than our highlight reel and occasionally rotten things happen, including break ups. I've only really shared one ex on social media in the past and I remember how difficult it was when we broke up, wondering if I should explain where he was gone or perhaps briefly take a break from being online so I could avoid the subject in case it arose. Followers used to comment asking me why I wasn't going on holidays and expressed concern when I didn't post frequently throughout the split. It was horrible having an extra pressure added to an already crappy scenario, but it's almost expected in the business I'm in. The nature of the internet puts a huge exterior strain on these situations, can make you feel overwhelmed and constantly reminded of the person you're no longer with regardless of your profile and industry. Respect is hugely important here. I would highly suggest not airing your dirty laundry or attacking your ex online, in my eyes nothing good can come from it. Of course, certain quotes and memes that you might see will be relevant and you're entitled to hint at what's going on, but shouting your turmoil from the rooftops will just make you feel more exposed and vulnerable and appear immature.

I also feel that no good can come from remaining friends with your ex on Facebook. Even if you've had an amicable split, seeing what he's doing every day, potentially seeing his new girlfriend or an inconsiderate status update can cause nothing but stress and in turn end the real life friendship you may be able to salvage. If you've ended on a good note perhaps let your ex know you plan on deleting him, that it's not being done out of malice, you just simply want both of you to be able to move on and you wish him well. If things have ended on a more turbulent note, all the more reason to break free from his updates and privatise your own as soon as possible. There will be photographs of you guys too and this is the really tough part. Do you keep them? Only to flick through them frantically everyday? Or do you delete them or untag yourself? The memories will remain in your mind, so do you really need the added torture of romanticising over that holiday in Portugal or your first Christmas together? If it doesn't help you it hinders you, so I say delete.

After Acceptance

Once you've made your list, accepted the fact it will take time to heal, refrained from contacting your ex and removed the majority of memories from your life, including that hoodie that smells like him, it's time to get out of those pjs and make progress.

Having a break up buddy who you can chat to throughout all stages of this process is essential. You need someone who knows the entire story of your relationship including how it ended, someone who is strong and will help you power through weak moments. Your chum of choice will need to be understanding and not bore or tire of your back and forth for some time. They will need to be willing to spend some time discussing your ex in lengthy detail, advise you repeatedly as to why you shouldn't call him and distract you with fun-filled activities. I'm blessed to have some amazing gal pals who were invaluable in the past. From popping round with chocolate or being my plus ones when the pain was too big a burden to bear alone at events, I'm eternally grateful for my friends and have since returned the favour when they themselves landed in similar situations.

In terms of going out with the girls, take your time on this one. Pushing yourself to go to a club to party and dance can lead to some break downs and worst of all drunk dialling. Alcohol can bring on more extreme emotions, so if you miss your ex sober you're going to miss him ten times more with ten tequilas in your system. When you're ready to brave a bop, make sure you hang out with responsible people who will look after you, ensure you don't get paralytic and that you are okay when a few tears should fall. Going out with single girls is fun because you're all in the same boat but don't give up on or avoid your pals who have partners. Eventually you need to learn to love again so don't become scornful or jealous of the happiness of others, because when you're happy again you'll want them to be happy for you too.

Exercise Out Emotion

Throughout my more recent break up I was strong enough to know and truly believe I would be okay, I simply needed time. I accepted the split and knew it was for the best, I knew there was no possibility of us ever getting back together and that clean break is often easier.

As a result I immersed myself in new projects to pass my time, heal and improve myself. One of those projects was joining a gym, possibly one of the best things I've ever decided to do, as it was the perfect time to really challenge my mind and body. I wanted to prove a point to myself, not my ex, that I was strong, that I was resilient and that I could do better than dwell on a sad inevitability. I'll speak in more depth about my previous experience with diet and fitness in Chapter 8, but in short let's just say I loathed exercise. I began my journey with a bad attitude to fitness and had a horrendous diet. A great starting point, I completely overhauled my mind and body and promised myself that every day I felt sad I would go to the gym. The gym can be an amazing escape from hardship or hell. When you're lifting heavy weights or sweating profusely in a cardio class it's relatively difficult to think about the demons that are causing your depression.

The sheer focus required when you push your body means your mind has very little time to drift away to dark places. After working out there's also lovely little things called endorphins that are released in your brain, replacing every sad cell with happy ones. After time, the body becomes addicted to the good hormones and requires more to function, thus making the whole task of going to the gym a positive one until the day you wonder how you ever hated it. If you can't face a Personal Trainer or individual workout session, why not try a Yoga or Pilates class that will allow you to simply stretch and breathe through the tough time? I found Body Balance amazing at the start because it was slow paced, still made me sweat and had a mindfulness session at the end to meditate and expend emotion. After time if you stick at your new routine and fuel yourself with the right food, your increased energy levels will in turn provide a sense of wellbeing and motivation to do more activities. Your new body will instill confidence and looking smoking hot when you bump into your ex can't hurt!

Find a New Hobby

If fitness really isn't your thing and you've at least attempted some form of exercise for a few weeks, then getting some sort of new focus is integral.

When we're younger our parents look after sending us to sports, activities and creative classes, which the majority of us give up in our adult lives. Work and life get in the way and we forget how fun and consuming a new pursuit can be. Whether it's something artistic like card making or painting, or more adventurous like rock climbing or surfing, spending a small amount of money on a new project can work wonders. When my anxiety was at an all time high my aunty bought me a grown up paint by numbers kit to take my mind off panic attacks and alleviate stress. Some people join Slimming World with a friend while others persuade a pal to come salsa dancing, heck you could even try speed dating. It really doesn't matter what you choose to take up, what matters is that you at least stick at it long enough to change your mindset and focus on the new, positive changes and additions to your life.

Put simply, the busier you are being happier the less time you have for being sad. Another bonus that comes with new activities is meeting new people. Some of whom could be a group of future friends or even a new man. If you're experiencing singledom for the first time the last thing you're probably looking for or thinking about is meeting anyone else but in time a door will open when you've shut your old one completely. There will come a time when dating again will be appealing and the more full your life is and the more handsome men taking part in your new hobby the better in order to keep your options open.

Getting Rebound Ready

Dating can be a dreaded task when you're newly single. Initially you will compare everyone to your ex and this can be a good or bad thing.

If your ex was amazing in every way in your eyes then no one will come close to the pedestal you currently have him on. If your ex was a pig, then dating can show you what you truly deserve and make you laugh at how you ever accepted previous behaviour. When it comes to dating, my motto is to keep your standards high and your expectations low. I've always had a certain standard and type, looks and personality wise, which has become even more fine tuned as I've matured. I don't waver from that standard or settle for anything less, but I remain open to different looks and characteristics that may suit me better. Keeping your expectations low is equally important. If you go into dating expecting to immediately find your perfect man you'll be sorely mistaken. It takes time to find the one, or even someone close to suitable so you need to be prepared to meet the good, the bad and the ugly and above all have patience.

When you've been hurt in the past, lack of trust can play a major part in avoiding dating altogether for fear of history repeating itself. When you give yourself to someone and they shatter your dreams of a future together, putting your faith in someone new is daunting to put it mildly. The opposite of love isn't hate, it's fear and fear can be the third wheel that destroys most new partnerships. Whether it manifests as insecurity or a defensive nature, a cold calculated view on love can prevent you from ever finding true happiness. At the end of the day, no one knows if something is going to work long term but you have to at least give it a chance. As you get older the warning signs are generally there and if things start to take a turn for the worse I suggest leaving before investing.

Learn to Be Open

If you've decided to take the plunge and begin exploring dating again then there are a few things to bear in mind. In terms of how you need to carry yourself, arriving with an open mind is essential.

As I touched on above, being open allows you to widen your definition of a compatible mate and prevents you from ruling out your set type. In the past I've been guilty of this and literally refused to date anyone shorter than 6.3" with black hair and strong cheekbones. This silly approach resulted in a string of model boyfriends with no ambition or chance of a future together. It took time to learn that he may not have a six pack but he could treat you like a princess and that ex of yours who had rippling abs and treated you like dirt suddenly isn't so appealing. If you can forget all of your past experiences and look at the person sitting across from you as a potentially new and exciting chapter in your life, you'll feel more at ease. I know lots of single women who are so overly critical that they see flaws in everyone they meet, meaning that they end up losing hope and becoming irritated by the dating process which should be fun and exciting. These women then get stuck in a rut where they become undesirable and needy, which men can smell a mile off. When they eventually start texting someone they like their patience has worn so thin that they become frantic if they don't hear back, or immediately assume the worst, in turn ruining something that never even had a chance to begin.

Staying calm, collected and somewhat guarded is the best combination. You need to have a strong no bullshit approach with a chilled outlook, you're in control of your desires and emotions and you can give away the snippets of information about yourself if you choose. Make sure you're honest with these nuggets though, because pretending you only want a hook up when really you're looking for a boyfriend will land you in a sticky situation. It's important to keep your cards close to your chest and not express deep and heavy feelings early on, which can scare someone away, but don't lie to yourself or him either.

Stranger Danger

Unfortunately you can't predict or plan for what might happen with the new bloke you've agreed to go for drinks with but you can have your wits about you in order to detect warning signs.

In the initial stages before meeting and during dating if he's reliable contact wise and seems to really want to talk to you then you're off to a good start. Flakey men only get worse with time and become incredibly unreliable. The issue here is that if you accept and allow flakiness early on then you can't complain about it six months in. The starting phase of any relationship generally determines and sets the scene for the rest of your time together, so in general what you allow will continue. If he only wants to text and never calls that's always a red flag in my books. The fact that he's not mature enough to pick up the phone and chat means he's not really interested in talking to you, willing to compromise on contact or worse has something to hide. Similarly if you only get a text from him when he's drunk at 2am on a Saturday then chances are he's only after one thing and not willing to make an effort outside of satisfying his desires. Early on, when feelings are detached, it's important to have your wits about you and treat dates like romantic interviews. If someone isn't fit for the job then they don't get the job offer, plain and simple. Unfortunately characteristics like jealousy and control usually only manifest after you're somewhat committed to someone so they are things to work on should they arise later on.

Attributes like anger, lying, or rudeness, which are more easily detected but can often only manifest a few months in, should also be addressed. One sad fact I've had to come to terms with is that a stranger can turn into someone special in your life, everything can go great with no warning signs and then the man can freak out. Whether he has emotional or commitment issues, whatever the reason, the guy that called you 14 times a day now wants to be on his own. Again this is something you deal with when you come to it and for me it's a case of better off knowing now rather than later.

Dating Dos and Don'ts

No one is perfect but traits like the following are pretty hard to get rid of so keep your eyes open for them. If your man treats the waiter with respect and has good manners, opens doors for you and offers to pay in the early stages then chances are he's a good egg.

Regardless of how modernised the worlds has become, traditional rules of dating are worth sticking to somewhat. Men should act like gentlemen and women should act like ladies. Even if you're one of the lads amongst your group of friends it's nice to make an effort and show some etiquette. This leads nicely onto alcohol. If you're a light weight or used to downing shots every weekend I would suggest having some self restraint on a first date. There's nothing worse than embarrassing yourself in front of someone you barely know and having to leave early because you're had one too many. A glass of wine or three will ease your nerves and highlight confidence but hold back on ordering any more. Conversation is so important early on because you're essentially selling yourself and deciding if you want to buy more time with him. The person wants to get to know the present you not your past.

Sure, some anecdotes and memories are fine but talking about your ex or past relationship can really put someone off. Your current values, goals, aspirations, likes and dislikes will either attract or dissuade your date. Make sure the conversation is balanced; no one likes a narcissist and only talking about yourself can come across as vain and disinterested. It's also extremely important that you start to find out about the person you're dating for your own benefit. For example, if your new man doesn't like animals and you have a zoo at home then there's an instant point of contention. The more you can find out during your romantic interview the better chance you both have of making a match.

Escape Route

If your date is arrogant or so far from what you're looking for that you know it will never work then it's also okay to call it a night and have a back up plan.

Meeting someone new is full of possibilities and it's important to prepare for the worst, so telling friends and family where you are and having an emergency phone call option is advised. You're perfectly within your right to explain to your date that you have to leave or that it simply isn't working for you and he's different to how you imagined. Chances are, if you're not feeling it he isn't either and sometimes it can just lack that special spark. Best case scenario, you have a new friend and worst case you never see him again and have to block his number. I've experienced plenty of dreadful dates in my time from a footballer who only spoke about his skills on the pitch

to a guy who was aggressive and arrogant to the point that I was forced to leave dinner. I think my most awkward date was one where I knew immediately I wasn't attracted to the guy, gave him every disinterested sign. I yawned, I was boring, I looked away at the bar, I fidgeted, I told him I didn't want a second drink and made up a story about having to work the following day so I could leave after a half hour. He lived near my house and wasn't drinking so dropped me home.

Instead of picking up on my negative energy he lunged in the car and forcefully tried to kiss me, which led to me embarrassingly banging my head off his window. He then sent me texts incessantly that night and for the next week or so until the point when I had to block his number. I've also been on a date with someone I initially didn't fancy whatsoever, who I ended up seeing for a few months! And I almost cancelled a date with someone who turned out to be very special.

Patience is Key

If you're lucky enough to have an awesome date then chances are you'll both discuss date two and know where you stand. Unfortunately it's not always that straight forward and things can be left on an ambiguous note.

Everything was amazing, you shared a kiss and he seemed so interested. Three days later, no text. Men love the chase of lusting after a girl only to get her on a date, enjoy their time and simply move on. Serial daters often become addicted to that new and fresh feeling and simply don't want anything more. As irritating as that sounds the reality is that it was never going to go anywhere from the start and you can stop wasting your time and energy now. Sometimes serial daters actually get into relationships, fall head over heels quickly without stopping to think what they've gotten themselves in for. Three months down the line after sharing three magic words they want to be single again and their habitual nature surfaces. This situation is ten times worse because feelings and future plans are involved. I don't believe serial daters lack emotion, unfortunately their selfish nature simply overrides and they move onto the next project leaving you wondering what the hell just happened.

In the game of love you'll meet plenty of different characters, who will open up a world of possibilities and learning curves. You may meet someone who lights a fire in you that you thought had burned out, someone who ends up fancying your best friend, someone who wants to take you travelling or someone who breaks your heart, the possibilities are endless. No matter what you're looking for, whether it's an ego boost, a husband or a bit of fun, give it time. Just like the healing process, searching for a soul mate isn't instantaneous. When you've built yourself up to be a strong independent person no one can knock your confidence and the right person will be worthy of your beauty when the time is right.

Chapter **5**

Accepting
Anxiety

That Familiar Feeling

Ironically, the day that I signed the contract for this book, I experienced my first panic attack in a long time.

That sickeningly familiar feeling of being overwhelmed, the adrenaline rush, the manic mixture of excitement and fear, the instant marvels and worries; so many differing emotions. I'm one of those individuals who feels everything and nothing completely. I'm a deep thinker, an over thinker, I think about every possible outcome and eventuality even if some of them are completely nonsensical. My tummy churns and flips with every positive or negative progression in my life and having experienced panic attacks in the past, my body remembers that fight or flight mode all too well. Some people publicly panic, they express fear openly, their breath quickens, their palms get sweaty, knees weak, arms are heavy... anyone remember that Eminem song?! Seriously though, I panic in private; I appear calm and collected, attentive and able, but inside I'm a ticking time bomb waiting to go off.

Sitting across from my warm, kind and friendly publisher that day I started to drift out of conversation and look towards the exit. My swallowing became difficult and I wondered if he noticed. Reaching for the water on the table to remind myself to cool down, literally, and that my swallowing mechanism was in fact working just fine, I concentrated on the words coming out of his mouth, even though the exciting news and plans ahead appeared muddled up in speech bubbles of doubt popping up in my peripheral vision. It took everything in my power to focus on my breath before making a bathroom beeline.

Beating Yourself Up

Ever since I began my blog my dream was to write a book and there I was signing a book deal and close to having a panic attack.

I instantly became annoyed at myself for not relishing in that moment; I wanted to take it all in and embrace the exciting opportunity in front of me, the one that I'd been working towards for so long, and yet all I could think about were the sensations in my body.

When you go long periods without panic life is dreamy, you almost forget the old you. The daily tasks that used to worry you are easy breezy and you can take on the world. The moment that familiar panic rears its ugly head, every sense of progress seems to come crashing down around you like a ton of bricks. Factually I am aware that I'm safe, that nothing bad is about to happen. In fact, nothing bad ever happens during or after an attack, apart from the surge of feelings and emotions and the drained aftermath that ensues. I think, for so many people who suffer anxiety, it's the feeling that they've failed themselves that prevails. Their strength washes away with every sharp breath and pounding heart beat. There's such a feeling of vulnerability that comes with anxiety; it inhibits day-to-day life, it affects your mood and the personality you portray to the world. You're exposed and waiting on the next attack or trigger. For those of you who have been following my blog for some time you may have already read one of my most popular articles to date, featuring my anxiety story. For those of you new to my experience, it goes a little something like this.

My First Attack

Up until the age of 24 I don't think I really understood anxiety or panic attacks. Now that I have experienced both I can say I have had panic attacks before, but they were by no means frequent, an issue, or something I feared would return.

So let's go back to the very first attack. Sitting across the table from my then loving, long-term boyfriend on a trip to Turkey, I was the picture of happiness; tanned, toned, in love and on holidays. We were in a busy restaurant about halfway through our holiday and in the midst of dinner I could feel myself drift out of the conversation. I began to feel a heightened awareness of everything from smells, and heat to sounds, yet I felt somewhat out of it. I wasn't really listening to what he was saying and I felt almost drunk and disoriented. My instant reaction was to drink water and go to the toilet. I sat in the loo trying to piece together what was happening my body, then the more I did so the more my body reciprocated and gave me more to think about and everything seemed to build. By the time I came out of the toilet I was upset and worried. My boyfriend questioned what was wrong and asked if I wanted to leave to go for a walk. I was scared I would faint, my thoughts were racing, I wanted to be alone yet wanted him near me and one thing was for sure I wanted out of that busy restaurant. So we walked and talked and he calmed me down. After about a half an hour or so I just crumbled and cried and felt an overwhelming sense of confusion and emotion. What had happened?

Feeling Like a Failure

I rang my mum in floods of tears every morning on that holiday, after numerous sleepless nights I had an overactive worried brain. She assured me that I was far from home, in humid weather and hugely stressed.

I never wanted my home and my bed so badly, I suppose I thought if I came home everything would be okay. That it was just the holiday I was on that was making me panic. But the night I arrived home, I had a panic attack, and the day after, and the night after that. I was so beyond devastated that I had failed, that I had no place to blame as the cause of panic. It was me, the panic was in fact inside me.

Wherever You Go, There You Are

The more I had high anxiety and attacks the more I found it hard to function. Everyday articles and emails became difficult to deal with as they reminded me of work and pressure.

Future plans seemed daunting and I questioned where I was in my life. Was I too old? So many questions and so many hurts overwhelmed me. The worry and the questions then brought on a severe sadness. After a panic attack you become drained, emotionally and physically. Your mind is tired from over thinking and your body is tired from pumping out all of that adrenaline. I won't bore you with every side effect, but even your digestive system works overtime during an attack, causing stomach cramps, gurgles and tension. Tired, sad, lonely and depressed the cycle of panic took hold of me; the more I was anxious the more I became depressed and the more I was depressed the more I became anxious. Would I be like this forever? Was I changing personality? Did I have a disorder? Did I need medication? Did I need help? Which came first, the panic or the sadness?

Asking For Help

My Fairy First Birthday was a momentous occasion for me in so many ways.

Over 700 of my readers came to support me at a huge event at one of the worst times in my personal life without them even knowing it. I spent the entire night holding it together. Would my readers know? Would I need to leave my own party? At the end of that event I bawled my eyes out and sobbed in the car home with my close friends and family. I just wanted to press pause on my life and fix this problem. From that moment on my family and closest friends were my rocks. They lifted my mood, continued to keep me laughing through the tears and offered help. I would fight this, but I wasn't going to be allowed do it alone. I began going for evening walks with my mum and auntie to clear my head, release endorphins and talk it out. I listened to other people's stories, I researched the issues I was experiencing. I wrote down my triggers, which I found to be unresolved emotional stress and over working, with post alcohol consumption and hormonal periods being times when anxiety was naturally higher. I began reading two books; *Wherever You Go There You Are* and *CBT For Dummies*. The first of which has been the greatest help, it explains the concept of Mindfulness, a process simply about being aware of your life in the now. Not the past or future, but right this moment. It guides you through practical meditation and breathing.

You CANNOT have a panic attack if you breathe correctly. Ever since I learned this fact if has been such a benefit and safety net for me. *CBT For Dummies* is more theory about why your thoughts provoke what they do, it helps you to realise the irrationality of the waves of panic that occur and shows you how to re think your thinking. I also went to a GP. A general check up and a few tears later I got all of my bloods checked and got the all clear. I was healthy in body, which made my mind rest a little easier.

Seeking Support

Every night on my journey back to health my mum read a page from a book called Journey To The Heart to me. I felt like a little girl being minded again, she would read it to me and stroke my hair and explain how everything was in fact going to be okay.

She told me how proud everyone was of me, how I didn't always have to work so hard, how beautiful I was and how I didn't have to do everything alone anymore or battle through pains and hurts that were nowhere near healed. I also visited a psychotherapist, which wasn't for me, in that I can talk and find it easy to detect my own triggers, and I simply didn't need to re hash old wounds. For me it was the immediate anxiety I wanted to tackle. But if you have unresolved issues it is definitely something I suggest.

Christmas wasn't as hard as I thought it would be that year; those close to me knew I was somewhat on edge but that almost made it okay to be okay. I went to my family home in West Cork, I didn't wear any make up and stayed in my comfy clothes. I read books, I walked down country roads, I bought lavender for my pillow and kept Rescue Remedy in my bag at all times. I did every basic thing I knew to do just that, bring me back to basics. I decided to no longer stay on technology and social media till all hours, working or posting and replying to mails. I stopped putting myself under pressure and took the time out to just heal myself. I didn't want to resort to medication, but that is most certainly an option for some, I just wanted to try everything else first.

Treating Your Triggers

So where am I today? Am I free from anxiety, no. Am I much better, more educated and more able to handle it? 100% yes.

Bar the book contact signing panic I experienced, I haven't had an actual attack in over a year, and although my anxiety is higher at certain times I'm aware of the signs now and what exacerbates my panic mode. If I'm sad about something exterior or due my period, for example, I will watch a film that will make me cry — sounds barmy, but I find letting the emotion out in a normal enjoyable way actually helps keep the panic at bay - it's like you're expending that pent up emotion.

Similarly, I watch something happy or listen to upbeat music to lift my spirits. If I don't feel like going out, I compromise and go for a walk instead. I call a friend or I go to bed early to allow sleep to work it's magic; sleep heals so many wounds and those things we overthink lying awake at night never seem half as bad in the morning.

Discussing my story so publicly was very difficult at the time. I was afraid my followers would see weakness and cracks in my strong social media presence. I felt exposed even though I had the choice and control over the information I shared. I had irrational worries that PR companies and fellow bloggers would look at me differently at events. Anxiety is very real and intrinsically linked to depression and depression is a dark hole that's hard to get out of when we forget to see the light. You can have the happiest life from the outside and still feel empty and sometimes it's just about being okay with that. I constantly gave myself grief, thinking to myself 'but I should be happy, I'm so lucky'. I've learned that we all put ourselves under huge pressure throughout day-to-day life and social media really exacerbates that. We're constantly looking at highlight reels and perfectly filtered newsfeeds that can make the tough times we experience pale in comparison.

From Feelings To Fears

When you're having a bad day, a tough time, a pause from panic mode, in my opinion the worst thing you can do is go online.

When you're a worry wart, Google is the never-ending tunnel of terrifying information. Any ailment that occurs during anxiety is generally a result of increased adrenaline and the mind over working, so researching why you feel dizzy or why your hands are numb will only bring on more worry when you read the varying and sometimes barmy explanatory search results.

Similarly, trawling through the photos of the gorgeous girls you follow on Instagram is going to make you feel down and depressed about their happy holiday, beautiful body or bearded boyfriend. Instead of looking outside of yourself in the just mentioned manner, it's far more important to look inside. What is it that's making you feel so scared, sad or alone? What brought on the panic this time? Was there a trigger? Are you stressed? Are you due your lady time? Have you eaten? Are you hung over? Did you just experience a break up? Sometimes there's a very obvious trigger that can spur anxiety, other times it can surface out of nowhere, and most of the time it can be a gradual build up of tension and triggers. The first and most obvious thing to do is to write down the potential triggers, followed by the feelings you're experiencing, and lastly the fears. By doing it in this order you can collate and investigate where the feelings are coming from so you can better understand why you're feeling them and then rationalise the fears at a time when you feel more at ease.

Pay Attention to Positives

Acceptance is also key when it comes to anxiety. If you try and fight something it will continue to return until the issue causing it has been dealt with.

You know when someone tells you not to look at something? All you want to do is look immediately. That's how I see anxiety and panic. If you tell it to go away, push it to one side and ignore it, your mind will naturally want to deal with it immediately and just like a head turn to look at that thing you've been told not to, your panic will heighten in a bid to tell you say 'LOOK AT ME NOW', 'Hey, I'm over here, DEAL WITH ME NOW'.

Obviously, upsetting and real-life triggers can't always be coped with immaculately, they are cards we're dealt and are sometimes out of our control. Natural negatives like a heart ache of any kind after experiencing a death, a pet loss, a change of career or break up, can trigger anxiety in the most strong and stable individual. Unfortunately, life will continue to throw these curve balls at you, you just have to learn how to hit them. It's also true what they say about whatever doesn't kill you making you stronger. I am ten times the woman I was after experiencing, dealing with and accepting anxiety. After time I was actually able to bring some humour into it and slag my irrational thoughts and laugh at the sensations in my body I deemed scary. Adding an element of light heartedness can really help your situation as it takes away from the deep, dark, heavy thoughts that can become addictive.

Don't Beat Yourself Up

What we can also control is our overall mentality, perception and thought process. It really is okay not to feel okay; life is full of ups and downs and we all handle them differently.

Berating yourself for having alternative feelings to those experienced by family and friends is only going to cause more damage and pressure which in turn leads to more panic, this full circle can become an additive cycle that's like a merry go round you feel that you can't get off of. Similarly, comparing yourself to someone who has never experienced a panic attack or anxiety is ridiculous. No two people are the same and it's our unique traits and idiosyncrasies that make us who we are. Some people turn to alcohol in a bid to manage stress, others aggression. Your alternative 'A' word is anxiety and it only makes you more interesting and empathetic. There's a freedom that comes with acceptance, knowing no one will judge your private thoughts or public panic, allowing the waves of emotion come and go, monitoring and probing what provokes your panic.

Banning the words 'should' and 'could' from your vocabulary, accepting what is going on now, being your own best friend, being good to others, going back to basics, treating your anxiety like a crime case and investigating it instead of knocking it or wishing it wasn't there will all help you. One of my favourite and most basic positive mantras is that everything will be okay in the end, and if it's not okay, it's not the end.

Just Breathe

Mentioned previously, one of the most basic yet comforting things I was informed of during the worst of my anxiety was that you physically cannot have a panic attack if you're breathing correctly.

Another interesting fact is that if you're able to speak and relay your panic to someone, everything is in working order. Even though you feel your breath quicken as if you can't breathe, the fact that you can express that means you're breathing just fine. We talk by making the air vibrate through breath and although this can seem like a scary side affect of panic, you're simply over thinking and manipulating something that usually comes naturally to the body.

For most people, the issue with breathing during anxiety attacks isn't actually the ability to inhale, it's the quick exhale that causes problems and panic. Prior to taking a deep breath you need to give a deep breath away, also known as exhaling. If you're shallow breathing through your chest, your body will get enough air but your mind will start to race. Essentially the equivalent of hyperventilating, that short sharp breath will tighten your chest leading to what feels like a pain in your heart, cause it to race and potentially create dizzy spells, blurred vision and tingling sensations. Some of the most common symptoms of 'panic attacks' are actually symptomatic of incorrect breathing as opposed to panic. If you knew that taking control of such a basic yet overlooked bodily function such as your breathing, would reduce the risk of anxiety and panic attacks, would you work on it? I certainly did and still do so every day.

This Too Shall Pass

Unfortunately, when anxiety subsides and we begin living a happy, carefree life again we forget all of the fantastic things we learned along the way.

During those dark and scary times we research, talk, and ask for help because we feel so rotten. We will do anything to feel better, to feel 'normal' again or to feel like us. I put huge pressure on myself to get back to the way I used to be before I ever had a panic attack so that I could forget the horrible experience and newly acquired and ingrained mechanism. However, life is all about change and adaptation and we are resilient creatures who grow and learn unconsciously every day through every triumph and every struggle. Without my experience I wouldn't have looked into myself, wanted to change and better myself, had a desire to help others or understood metal illness. When we feel happy we tend to put said information and positive progression into a box that we lock and hide away for fear of remembering the bad times. We want to move forward with confidence and leave the past behind.

The thing is, if you don't continually work on yourself throughout the good times, the bad times can creep back unexpectedly and you're less able to deal with those dreaded demons when they return. Preparing yourself for the bad times whilst maintaining a positive attitude is the best way to preserve peace. During my learning curve I wrote down a list of ten things I was thankful for everyday. No matter how I was feeling I reminded myself how lucky I was and accepted my current state as a moment that was temporary.

Mindful Minutes

Mindfulness has been a magic method for my situation. Put simply, mindfulness is a mental state achieved by focusing your awareness on the present moment, being right here, right now, accepting where you are, taking it in and calmly acknowledging and accepting your feelings, thoughts, and bodily sensations.

Some people find meditation extremely difficult, myself included. If you have the capacity and habit of overthinking, being told to sit in the same spot for half an hour and not think seems ludicrous and downright impossible. However, just like exercising in the gym, these conscious acts exercise the mind over time. When you enter the gym for the first time you would never be expected to squat 60kg right away with perfect form and technique. Similarly, attempting to sit down to mediate and expecting it to work perfectly the first time, clear your mind and solve all your problems is setting yourself up to fail and become disheartened. Mindfulness is more of a daily therapeutic technique, which can be incorporated and introduced into your routine bit by bit. Whether it's five minutes of your afternoon spent working on your breathing or ten

minutes before bed, day-by-day and week by week, you will decrease your rapid thoughts and increase your ability to concentrate on being present. The first time I tried to meditate I was beyond frustrated. I spent the entire time trying to stop my wandering thoughts and wanted to give up after five minutes.

The thing about mindfulness is that you don't have to push your thoughts away, instead you allow them, embrace them and let them pass, gently reminding yourself to come back to the present. The benefits of gradually introducing these mindful minutes into your daily life far outweigh the initial difficulties you may experience. After time you'll be amazed at how focused your mind can become at simply being present, and accepting everything just as it is. When I began to progress I found myself becoming quite emotional during my meditation, it was as if I was expending the pent up panic and stress in a positive natural way. The adrenaline and anxiety seemed to lessen and a sense of calm began to take place.

Learning To Unplug

Mindfulness also incorporates a method called the body scan. Another way of training your attention and deflecting from worried or stressful thoughts, the body scan puts you in touch with various body parts in a bid to further practise being present.

There are lots of apps available that run through mindful methods like this with soothing serene step by steps, I personally love one called 'Headspace'. The body scan can be carried out anywhere you can lie down; on the ground, inside or outside, or my personal favourite, in bed at night before sleeping. I'm guilty of working till all hours and forgetting to switch off, I also used to leave my phone on at night meaning the temptation to access technology was all too real. Like so many who scroll before they sleep, the light in our devices tricks the brain into thinking it's day time, thus keeping us wide awake. If I see something inspiring before bed the last thing I want to do is sleep; I want to write down ideas and work. If I see something sad, it plays on my mind and I over think situations, and if I see a comment on social media that's negatively directed at me or someone I know, I feel anxious and uneasy.

I also used to leave my phone on at night meaning the temptation to access technology was all too real.

So instead of flicking through Facebook before bed, why not invest in a good mindful app and try out a bedtime body scan. I know every time I do one I drift into a more settled slumber and wake up feeling well rested and refreshed.

Whether it's helping out at home, offering someone a lift, joining a friend at the gym when you really don't feel like going, being mindful of the birds in the morning or how the trees sway in the wind. If you go a step further and decide to donate to charity or spend time with the elderly you would be surprised how these conscious actions begin to take that heavy weight from your own anxious shoulders and create a more carefree and appreciative outlook on life.

Reaching Out to Others

After sharing my story on anxiety, for example, I began to look outside myself. Instead of wallowing in my own circumstantial situation I decided to utilise the platform I'd created to benefit and potentially help others.

I swore to myself that if my article touched just one of my readers suffering from panic attacks my job was done. After all, what's the point in having thousands of followers if all I post is make up selfies and a fabulous life? The truth is, life isn't peachy all the time, in fact far from it, and I'm human just like each and every one of my beautiful followers and I owe them, and you, the good, the bad and the ugly.

The feedback I received, and still receive to this day after sharing my story and utilising that vulnerable period in my life is astounding. Mental illness is a very prevalent issue in a society where there are more and more reasons to stress and spiral into an episode of doubt and self-loathing. As a community with individual online platforms we need to share our thoughts and feelings in a bid to not only clear our own heads but also to step outside ourselves and help others. So many young girls and women have felt the same way as I did. They experienced the exact form of panic, they thanked me for expressing things they didn't have the words or energy to. They too had difficulty swallowing or had a fear or flying, they wanted to curl up and sleep to avoid reality but instead were brave enough to mail me and share their story, which in turn helped me. And here we are full circle.

After all, what's the point in having thousands of followers if all I post is make up selfies and a fabulous life? The truth is, life isn't peachy all the time...

Chapter **6**

Body
Beautiful

My Shape Story

I've always considered myself body confident. As I reflect on the varying shapes and sizes I've been and embraced over the years, there was no time I utterly loathed my build to the point where it affected my stature and poise.

Whether I was a slim and lanky teen wearing a size 8, or a curvy and full-figured size 14 at the age of 25, I knew how to carry myself. Like any girl, when I look in the mirror I still find flaws; if certain light hits the back of my thighs I can see cellulite. I have some stretch marks on my inner thighs from weight gain and loss and my boobs aren't as perky as they used to be. Standing at 5"10, I was generally taller than most of my peers, which used to bother me somewhat. At the end of my school years when we started to socialise I hated wearing heels for fear of towering over people like a giant, not to mention the fact that Irish men are known to lack in the height department. Owing to the fact that I was a combination of tall and curvy, I was always referred to as Amazonian, which I despised. Ironically, now I take it as a compliment.

My height is considered a bonus in the modelling industry and my curvier frame has managed to book me jobs in a niche department. My height and frame make me stand out from a crowd and I can always find my friends in a nightclub. I guess I try not to spend too much time dwelling on my flaws and worry more about my character and where I'm at in life. I firmly believe, in terms of your body, that there are always ways and means to tweak and change things you dislike. If I'm unhappy with weight gain, I need to review my diet and work out more. If I've lost muscle I need to do less cardio and lift heavier weights. Naturally there are certain things I can't change, but instead of focusing on them and becoming progressively more insecure, I merely accept them and look to things I love about myself instead. Aesthetics and positive body image have an important role to play in our happiness, if you learn to love yourself from the inside then everything else is an exterior, less important trait. I firmly believe that if you value looks and aesthetics over personality, you'll live a very unfulfilled and unhappy life. People are so much more than the bodies they live in and as soon as you start to appreciate how wonderful that body you live in is, you'll start to enjoy decorating it instead of tearing it down.

I firmly believe, in terms of your body, that there are always ways and means to tweak and change things you dislike. If I'm unhappy with weight gain, I need to review my diet and work out more.

Love Yourself List

If you're really struggling with body confidence and find it hard to see the positives in how you look and feel then you need to begin with an exercise I like to call the love yourself list.

We, especially as women, tend to overlook the amazing things about our bodies and focus on the negative, more unsightly attributes. Instead of appreciating the hugely amazing qualities and abilities our bodies have, we nit pick at the minor issues that we consider flaws. When we're younger we want to look older and apply make up in a manner that makes us look more mature. When we're older we try and emulate a more youthful look and take a few years off our appearance. Slimmer girls crave curves and curvier girls admire more athletic builds. The age old wanting what you can't have, grass greener syndrome is detrimental. This constant desire to be something we're not in this moment can cause grave unhappiness.

The age old wanting what you can't have, grass greener syndrome is detrimental.

Instead of looking at unachievable looks and figures we need to spend more time genuinely appreciating and making the most of our own beauty. The girl who dislikes her thin lips probably has beautiful eyes and the girl who wishes she had green eyes probably has a perfect pout. I urge you, as an experiment, to list at least 10 things you love about yourself looks-wise, because I guarantee you would find it easy to list 10 things you hate. To get you inspired, here is my list. Bear in mind that this exercise should not be considered vain or fuelled by ego, it's designed to make you refocus and prevent dwelling on negative thoughts. I actually struggled to get beyond point five, so the fact that this exercise really made me think about my body and the parts I like is the reason it will benefit you too.

My LOVE **YOURSELF** LIST

1 EYES

I have big green eyes. Only 2% of the population have this eye colour, meaning I'm in a minority, and the large shape allows me to apply lots of different eye looks. I can hold eye contact with the ones I love and see beautiful things around me.

2 NOSE

I have a relatively delicate nose, which lots of people have complimented me on. I have my mum's nose and it reminds me of her. I've never broken it, don't have any lumps or bumps, it suits my face shape and I can smell delicious food and flowers with it. Oh, and it helps me breathe.

3 LIPS

I have big lips that suit my big eyes. They're great for talking, eating and kissing and they stay soft year-round. I can play around with and apply lots of fun lip colours.

4 SKIN

I have an olive skin tone meaning I tan easily, hold a colour year-round and have a combination skin type. I don't have any obvious ageing and my skin is very soft and smooth to touch.

5 BOOBS

I've always had big boobs, they suit my curvy frame and balance my body. They make me feel sexy and men love them. When I have children, I'll be able to breast feed with them.

6 WAIST

My waist is the smallest part of my body. When I gain weight my waist remains small and when I lose weight it's accentuated. My waist creates an hourglass figure. My waist protects my vital organs and is the easiest place to tone.

7 HIPS

My hips are wide and womanly and keep me in proportion. One day when I decide to have a family, my hips will be the ideal child-bearing size. When I hold toddlers they sit perfectly on my hips, like a shelf.

8 THIGHS

I have strong, chunky thighs. My quads are prominent and I have good muscle definition. My thighs help me squat and leg press heavy weights and helped me with horse riding when I was younger. I can walk.

9 ANKLES

I have very small ankles which look extended when I wear heels. My ankles are feminine and delicate, but strong enough to hold my frame when I stand.

10 FEET

Although I loath feet of any kind (one of my irrational fears) I have quite pretty and girly feet. People have commented on how nice they are when I get my nails done or expose them on holidays and they're great for popping into pretty heels.

Appreciate Actions

Moving on from your love yourself list, hopefully you can begin to appreciate just how amazing your body is. Whatever your list contains, those are ten parts of you that are imperfectly perfect.

For every ten you find, I guarantee loved ones around you could add at least ten more. The moment you start to truly appreciate what your body is capable of is the moment you stop shaming yourself. Appreciating what your body can do is an excellent way to forget the less important things you've been wasting your time focusing on. Every body part has a purpose and looking beautiful is just the beginning. There are people on this earth who suffer horrendous illnesses that affect their body and regular functionality. From people who have lost limbs to those with extreme skin issues, chances are you have it lucky. That pimple you keep picking at and complaining about is nothing compared to someone who suffers from acne. Those boobs you wish were bigger or smaller are a blessed feature those who have suffered from breast cancer appreciate now more than ever. As extreme as it sounds, these comparisons can really bring you back to reality and start to make you take charge of your thoughts. If you genuinely have something to complain about or an illness that you're suffering from right now then I empathise with you. I guarantee you love your body now more than ever and envy those who seem to have it easy.

The more you complain and take things for granted the more things worthy of complaint will come your way. Releasing your body hatred can be exhilarating to say the least, by simply adjusting your inner dialogue you're taking the first step. Instead of using words like 'hate' when describing your arms, for example, say you love your legs out loud. Try to focus on all the amazing things your body has done for you and how magical it is. Instead of thinking about how bloated you are during your lady time, why not wonder at how marvellous it is that your body controls your hormones and is preparing for having a child. Aside from the air we breathe, your body produces things like oxytocin, which calms, fights disease and reduces stress. The more mindful you are about your body's capabilities the less likely you'll be to berate it.

Stop Shaming

One thing I've learned from putting myself in the public eye is how quick women are to body shame. Personally, I'll never understand the desire to judge someone else's shape or lifestyle, but it's such a common occurrence I've had to learn to witness, defend and deal with it.

Unfortunately, as a result of things like sensationalised images on magazine covers and online stories about how a certain celebrity has gained or lost weight, we as a society seem to think it's natural and acceptable to gossip and pass comments on others. Instead of feeling sorry for said celebrity as to what they may be going through in order for their weight to have fluctuated, or instead of considering how happy they may be in their new size, we are taught to focus on flaws like skin folds and scrutinise areas like thighs. Judging strangers has become normalised and we seem to do the same to individuals online, whether they're bloggers or make up artists, or anyone who showcases their trade on social media for the world to see.

I've experienced comments about my weight and figure in the past and 99% of it has come from women, which is the worst part. Men tend to sexualise images or have a preference for curvier frames and so they comment on weight loss or transformative images, explaining how they liked the girl better before. Women on the other hand scrutinise facial features, style choices, weight gain or loss and everything in between. Although I'm generalising here, I feel I've collated enough experience in this area to speak for a vast majority. When you look at images online it's very easy to forget the real person behind the camera. We appreciate the make up skills of a selfie, like how clothes are accessorised, dislike the way someone chooses to style their hair or how they pair their shoes. With this judgmental break down comes a certain lack of empathy and the person is somewhat treated as a visual instead of an individual with feelings. When you look at people with a larger following they tend to experience the most hate. I've had blogger friends with naturally slim frames bashed about their bones and similarly fellow curvy models mocked about their bigger bums. If you feel the need to tell someone what you think about their shape or size, try and address your reasoning behind it. Will you hurt the person receiving the comment? Would you say it to their face? And most importantly, would you like to be commented on in the same manner? The sooner we start to think seriously about the way we treat celebrities or social media personalities, the less likely we are to self hate and judge those who walk by us on the street.

I've experienced comments about my weight and figure in the past and 99% of it has come from women, which is the worst part.

Plus Sized Models

As a plus sized model, a certain demographic of curvy women follow me for fashion tips and to appreciate the confidence I exude online. I promote the love of lumps and how to embrace a fuller figure.

With that, I also experience the odd troll who feels I'm too big to be considered a fashion model or too small to be deemed plus size. Prior to my fitness transformation I was a full size 14 and placed in the plus size bracket. I was happy and confident in my body but my diet was unhealthy and I rarely exercised. For those unfamiliar with modeling, the general categorisation is that sizes UK 12 and above are considered plus size. Depending on the frame, UK 10 and below is a standard fashion model size. I now fall somewhere in the middle, a size 10-12, I still have a curvy frame with a big bust and bum meaning I can't be considered fashion but I'm not exactly plus size either. I didn't transform my body, lose weight or gain muscle for my industry, I did it for my health and well-being and allowed my body adjust according to the positive changes I made. I'm signed with three agencies at the moment, one in Dublin, one in Belfast and one in Capetown. I've been booked for TV, print, catwalk and presenting jobs based on my current look and size. I'm now getting more work than ever because I fall into the in between category and can apply for fashion and plus size jobs, but this has caused concern for some of my followers.

I suppose because a small minority of original followers loved my bigger body, they feel somewhat cheated by my decision to tone up and tighten my frame. A vast majority of people don't feel it's right that I'm considered curvy because they see plus size as a larger shape. My own confidence and body image is better than ever but I've definitely had knocks throughout this change. After breaking up with an ex, he commented on how I was better before I lost weight and that my boobs had changed. Already conscious of how my boobs weren't as full or perky, said comment really affected my mindset. I quickly slapped myself on the wrist and reminded myself of how I wasn't putting all of this work into my diet and fitness to please my ex or anyone else for that matter. This was a journey and decision I made to better myself, my mind and my body.

A vast majority of people don't feel it's right that I'm considered curvy because they see plus size as a larger shape.

Embrace The Skin You're In

Having worked in the modelling industry from the time I was in my early twenties, I've grown from feeling insecure and shy to becoming confident with how I look.

I'll never forget my first catwalk show; I was the only plus size model amongst five other slim girls. Instead of standing out in a good way I felt like everyone saw me as the big one. When I arrived backstage to try on my items for the show my entire rail was a size 12. At the time I was a full size 14 and immediately panicked at the thought of trying to fit into a section that was far too small. I attempted the first dress, which fit my hips and waist fine but wouldn't zip at the side of my bust. Mortified, I informed the stylist I was in fact a size 14 on my portfolio and that the size 12 rail would be too small. I was humiliated at having to explain my own size and felt almost apologetic for not being able to squeeze into garments without bursting buttons. The stylist was unhappy and said we didn't have time to get any new sizes and that I would simply have to make it work. Red faced, I tried my best to do just that, whether it was placing my arm over open zips or adding a jacket, I walked that show more uncomfortable than I've ever been. As a result of feeling fat, frumpy and the odd one out I was miserable and went home to cry that evening. Instead of embracing the fact that I was a curvy model booked for bigger sizes, I felt like I had entered the wrong career path. Was I cut out for situations like this? Was it worth the money? I was always confident in my shape but that experience alone made me question everything.

Instead of embracing the fact that I was a curvy model booked for bigger sizes, I felt like I had entered the wrong career path.

Another similar scenario occurred when I was doing a job on TV and was handed a pair of white linen trousers, again a size 12. In general most stylists will bring two sizes if an item is a tight fit or if they're unsure of a model's exact sizing. White linen is a material I would never wear to begin with as it accentuates my width and does the opposite of flattering my figure. I explained I was a size 14 and that the linen would almost burst at the seams if I attempted to squeeze into them. The stylist looked at me like I had caused the biggest inconvenience to her day, huffed, puffed and made a call to get someone to order a size 14 from their store. The whole morning was uncomfortable and I left questioning my career as a model once more. Instead of flaunting my curves I was constantly being reminded of how the industry was still the same and I was being treated like a slimmer model yet an outcast.

Every Body is Beautiful

Thanks to social media, plus size modelling was on the rise and agencies were starting to embrace, accept and include larger girls. Instead of being treated like a nuisance we were getting more job opportunities because we were few and far between.

I began to collect more experience on catwalk shows that went well, wore garments that fit in photo shoots and began getting booked for lingerie slots on TV which was a first for a fuller frame. As I matured in the industry and focused on my own work, taking modelling as a side-line earner, I appreciated the odd jobs I got but stopped being affected negatively by them. I enjoyed my time modelling and stood up for myself if I was treated any way negatively. My own social media following was growing dramatically at this point and big name brands like Primark and Boohoo began sending me items to model for their websites. The more styled pieces I featured on my own website the more job bookings I got and the more my agency supported my work.

Now at a size 10/12, I have more choice when it comes to modelling jobs, but I never lost weight to conform or fit in. My hourglass shape will always fall into the plus size category by virtue of the fact that my boobs and hips are large and my waist is small. I've learned to love my curves because they make me stand out, they've aided my career and make me feel womanly. I also appreciate smaller frames, more sporty physiques and bigger girls. Embracing the skin you're in allows room to appreciate people who are different and admire attributes you may not have. Once you accept your natural shape and make the most of it nothing can knock who you are, how you feel about yourself or anyone else. Having confidence in your size is the perfect power, and far outweighs standardised perfection. Having lost weight, I occasionally deal with stylists who now claim I'm too small to be plus size, which has taught me that you simply can't win. I am who I am, in this moment and I accept that.

Think Like a Man

Being immersed in a bitchy industry over the years, I've noticed how women tend to find negatives about how they look and judge other women on similar traits.

In general, men don't notice the flaws and insecurities we have. Why? Because they're so busy swooning over your fabulous face, stroking your soft skin or admiring your beautiful bum. We break down our bodies and pick out tiny blemishes and defects we deem disgusting. Men tend to look at the overall picture, like a painting and how it makes them feel. If your overall beauty makes them feel fuzzy then chances are they haven't noticed that stretch mark on your stomach. A woman who is skin and bone or overweight can still be sexy. When you look in the mirror, you become familiar with your beauty, you become accustomed to picking out parts you dislike. You don't look at yourself for the first time, you don't see yourself animated or alive. Have you ever come back from the hairdressers with a new do, only for your partner to just say you look 'nice'? You expect him to comment specifically on the additional highlights but he just gives you a generalised compliment. That's because he just generally finds you attractive in that moment, yet we get insulted when they don't spot the specific difference.

Men tend to look at the overall picture, like a painting and how it makes them feel. If your overall beauty makes them feel fuzzy then chances are they haven't noticed that stretch mark on your stomach.

We use lotions and potions every day and night and often endure procedures that men deem excessive. You could spend hours styling your hair for a night out and men will notice one of two things. Your hair is either up or down. Regardless, your face still looks pretty. Pale women love wearing fake tan because it makes them feel better, all that men notice is how bad it smells and the stains on the sheets. I know so many women who are afraid to go bare-faced with their other half in the morning, yet the man in their life prefers the natural version anyway. I used to have an aversion to being seen in the gym, red faced and sweaty, mortified if I bumped into an ex. The strangest thing is, men find fit girls incredibly sexy and instead of seeing a shiny beetroot face they see a strong girl who works out and the leggings that make your booty look amazing. Crows feet, smile lines, roots, split ends, tummy rolls, cellulite, uneven eye liner, chipped nails. Guess what? They don't notice, and perhaps we should take a leaf out of their lack of concern because perhaps those things don't matter. Sure it's important to maintain yourself and feel sexy, but on your off days please be kind to yourself and just embrace being you, because that in itself is beautiful.

Protect Your Circle

Surrounding yourself with positive people is a huge factor when it comes to body confidence. Although we can find inner strength and assurance, hanging around with body shamers and negative nellies can impact on your inner peace.

If you're fragile about your figure or easily influenced by opinions then you need to take a look at your circle. Let's face facts, girls can be nasty and one little snide remark about your body can really play on your mind. Perhaps your friend is insecure about how she looks and feels and is deflecting her thoughts. Either way it's no excuse and you need to address the issue. Try to be compassionate in how you approach it because judgmental people are made, not born. There is a reason why they feel the need to comment on your body or try to knock you from your positive place. Empathise with this and try to understand where they're at in that moment in time. If your friend continues to make you feel bad about yourself or less than beautiful in their company then you need to look at pulling away. Similarly, if you're in an unhealthy relationship with a man who makes you feel less than worthy, comments on your weight or bullies you, I would suggest removing him from the equation immediately. I've seen so many skinny girls go out with men who have big beer bellies, yet those men will comment on the fact that their girlfriend has gained a few pounds. This control and manipulation can lead to eating disorders and more. Life is too short to envelop yourself in people who want to knock you, so try to take it as a life lesson and learn from it. Be thankful that you're in a position where you don't feel the need to put anyone else down and are confident enough to walk away from something damaging.

If you have to prove your worth to someone, change how you look to suit them or lose strength in order to let them dominate the relationship dynamic, then that's not a relationship worth having. Getting to know new people is a great way to practise confidence and believe in yourself again, especially after an emotionally abusive relationship. If you believe in yourself you set the tone for initial contact with someone and they will see you as the person you put forward. Therefore being strong and confident, with enough vulnerability to not come across as cocky or egotistical, will attract like-minded individuals.

Perfecting Posture

After working on yourself from the inside out there are so many other simple ways to improve confidence. Standing tall with my shoulders back and head held high is how I enter a room, no matter how I'm feeling inside.

Emulating confidence through your posture and gait is a fantastic way to build self-esteem, make an entrance and give out good vibes. If you walk into a room with your head down, with eye contact to the floor and sloping shoulders, you not only appear unsure of your own identity but also unapproachable and unfriendly. Having an open stance that's powerful can make you feel better about yourself and create a presence that's confident even if it's only a temporary illusion. The more you practise standing tall and walking with assurance, the quicker you'll start to feel the certainty you may be lacking. After time, walking into a room filled with people, knowing you're worthy will compound just that. You simply cannot be body confident if you don't hold your body in a confident way. If you walk around with a lethargic gait the last thing you'll feel is empowered. Factually, your body also looks better when it's held upright. Pulling your shoulders back narrows your frame, elongates your neck and complements your shape. Rounding your shoulders pulls everything downwards and even adds inches to your waist. If having good posture doesn't come naturally to you then working out can really help. As I will be discussing in Chapter 8, fitness can greatly improve your body confidence.

Working out will also actively build up the muscles required for good posture. For example, when weight lifting, you're working on the agonist and antagonist muscles evenly in isolated areas like the back. This will balance out your body and make it easier to pin your shoulders back without consciously thinking about it. Having a strong core also helps your mid-section stay long and extended as opposed to curved and bent over. Sometimes when you're stressed and lacking confidence, your body can be stiff. Practising stretches is a great way to be mindful of how your body feels, improve the way it performs and in turn help your posture. The better your body feels on the inside the better it will look on the outside. The better you look on the outside the better you feel on the inside and so it comes full circle.

Stand Against Shaming

We live in a fast-paced world where everything nowadays is online. So many people are concerned with who is wearing what and what eyeshadow they're using.

People update their accounts in a bid to gain followers and as a result leave themselves open to a variety of opinions from strangers. These opinions can wreak havoc on our minds and insecurities. People seem to have forgotten what inner beauty is and focus solely on aesthetics. As a result, body image is somewhat distorted and held at such a level of importance that lip size is discussed more than someone's heart and how they handle situations.

I've dealt with body shaming first hand and I know how badly it can upset and affect your mindset. No matter how strong I've become, that one negative comment stands out amongst a thousand compliments. I've cried over my body and wished I were less curvy. I've prayed for an alternative shape in the past and I've had to work hard to truly find and accept myself. We need to stand together and fight body shaming and make room for self-love. God forbid someone posts something positive about their progress or says they adore their body. For whatever reason self-love is frowned upon by so many insecure individuals. It's seen as vain and narcissistic, when the reality is it's something to be admired. No one knows the battle each and every one of us has endured to finally love themselves and it's simply not okay to knock it. The sooner we embrace body confidence and commend ALL shapes and sizes the world will be a better place. So why not wake up today and compliment yourself in the mirror? Take a look at that love yourself list and remember how gorgeous you are. Why not give someone a random compliment, even if they're a stranger on the street? The more you project happiness the happier you'll feel. The less you focus on the negatives the more room there is to see and appreciate positives. If you truly dislike something about your body, change it. Whether it's working out, getting a treatment or adjusting your mindset, then do it. If you genuinely feel you have an issue with body image or an eating disorder then seek help. Speak to someone outside your circle that you can trust and confide in. Express your thoughts, write them down and work on them. We only have one body for the rest of our lives so why not start loving yours today.

Chapter **7**

Fashion
Fixers

Rebellious Rocker

My first real experience experimenting with fashion was at the tender age of 14. Like most teens, I wanted to express myself through my clothing and as difficult as it is to imagine now, I was a hybrid between a tomboy and an alternative rocker.

I went to Metallica concerts and listened to niche artists like Tool and A Perfect Circle, I hung out at underground gigs and fancied indie artists. In terms of my appearance and beauty regime I somewhat destroyed my natural look. I regularly dyed and chopped my hair, going from an angled bob to long locks that graduated from a harsh black colour into dip-dyed fire engine red. I had piercings and wore strong, thick Amy Winehouse angled liner and reached for the tweezers far too often, leaving my poor brows with a sperm-like shape. I hung out with fellow hipsters in Temple Bar, which is full of shops that suited my style back then. I enjoyed vest tops with zipper details, denim flared jeans with the most unflattering fit and big chunky boots. I think one of my most vile fashion choices to-date was this long length woolen, multi-coloured coat with tassels down the front. I wore that coat to death and thought that it was the epitome of gorgeous grunge.

I cringe even thinking back to those days and would be hard pushed to find photographic evidence of my 'alt' attire. I was tall and lanky with a relatively large bust and I did nothing to flatter my figure; I hid every curve I hated and tried to play up the androgynous look. Looking back, I was enjoying an experimental stage but my fashion sense was lacking and it showed in my poor punky picks and posture. Although I now loath the look I had back then, I thought I rocked it at the time and that's all that matters in the moment, regardless of the hideous evidence years on. I loved playing around with different styles and allowing my mood to manifest itself through my clothing. Even though that style is something I wouldn't dream of portraying now, I had an eye for piecing things together and I wasn't afraid of playing around with textures, mental colours or details. I also loved customising items, whether it was ripping sections of my tops and adding safety pins to close them back together, or sewing random buttons onto pockets to give them a unique finish. I didn't accept standardised fashion and I made the most of my token rebel look.

From Grunge to Girly

Fast forward a few years and I had grown out of my hideous hair and thrown away my flairs and graduated into a far more girly style. I wore powder pink playsuits and white shirts with mini hearts on them.

My hair was a natural brunette shade, reaching past my shoulders and almost always straightened with a GHD. I discovered havens like TopShop and began buying magazines to try and emulate their fashion features. I also started to show off my figure a little bit more instead of shying away from exposing my long legs and covering up my chest. I accepted the fact that I was tall, wore high heels with pride and stopped hating my bigger boobs as a result of my body balancing out a bit more. I kicked my nervous nail biting habit and grew them, painting them a different colour daily. I even saved some money to get manicures and had my brows professionally shaped. I adored accessories and started to build quite a sparkle selection. No matter what I was wearing, I would match my earrings or rings, I even went as far as bringing perfume bottles that were the same shade as my bag. I was somewhat obsessive compulsive about combining items and felt completely uncoordinated if the simplest thing was out of order, such as having gold buckles on my hand bag if I was wearing a belt with silver buckles. That still irks me to this day, unless I'm intentionally mixing metals. I started to put money aside for clothes and invested in the start of my shopping habit.

I accepted the fact that I was tall, wore high heels with pride and stopped hating my bigger boobs as a result of my body balancing out a bit more.

From the age of 18 I lived for the weekend when I could put pieces together and head out with my friends. I played around with make up and realised my proficiency in this area. My once angled eye liner became more delicate, I played around with smoky shadows, applied false lashes for a fluttery effect and lashed on lip gloss. My style had progressed into a far more flattering, fiercely feminine look, and with my new wardrobe came tons of confidence. It was around this stage that I realised how much the items you wear can enhance your mood and personality. I began to embrace brighter colours, which made me happy and only wore black in work. When I would wear darker hues during winter, I made sure my scarves or shoes still made a statement. I put a huge effort into getting ready every day and still enjoy those moments every morning.

Settling On a Style

From my early twenties up to the present, I would consider my style flirty and feminine, but I've moved away from following trends to finding my own style, which I was consider classy, sexy and colourful.

The structure of my outfits has naturally matured and I love playing around with shapes and balance. I like neutral tones and simplistic basics. I adore monochromatic looks with an edge and switch up my style to a girly gown at events. I can go from biker chic to glam gal in the same week and I regularly reach for my relaxed attire, which consists of a plain white tee, ripped jeans and Converse. I know what flatters my body shape and I've learned which items to avoid. My body has gradually changed over the years from tall, slim and lanky into slim and curvy and on to a much fuller figure and now a fit and healthy frame. My college years involved partying and eating junk food, which led to gradual weight gain. As a result I learned to adapt my attire and conceal the areas, or lumps and bumps, I disliked and showcase the ones I did. I stopped comparing myself to my friends' figures and learned how to work with my own. It was during this time that I really appreciated the effect fashion can have on your mind set in terms of body confidence.

The wrong outfit can make you feel frumpy and the right pair of heels can get you through the worst of weeks. Throughout my early twenties and up to now, I've also learned how to adapt my budget when it comes to expanding my wardrobe. I went from a rocker with a €20 weekly allowance who relied on raiding my mum's sewing kit, to a late teen working a part-time job, spending her earnings on dresses for the weekend. I then progressed to a college girl, tight on money and forced to source the best bargain buys, to a working woman who always allocates a certain amount each month to styling high street items and investing in classic pieces that will last. I also make the odd designer splurge every now and then, saving up for things I know will stand the test of time and work with my wardrobe.

Taste Over Trends

Regardless of your budget, there are ways to dress in the way you desire. Once you are inventive and have good taste, your money situation shouldn't matter too much.

Whatever your age there are certain styles you'll be drawn to and want to try out, the important thing to remember is that not all trends and styles will suit you. For example, flowing tops that gather under the bust make me look pregnant so I avoid them like the plague. Knowing your shape and working with it instead of against it is an important starting point when it comes to

fashion. Dressing appropriately for your age and the occasion is also key; it's nice to express yourself and showcase your sense of style without looking conventional but wearing a club dress in the work place isn't ideal!

Discovering your shape should be relatively easy; knowing your measurements is key here. Are you an apple shape, top heavy with killer legs? Or a pear with a beautiful booty? Are you a lean, column shape and amazing athlete? Or, like me, do you fluctuate from a full to neat hourglass? Whatever your size, knowing how to highlight your positives and detract from your negatives is invaluable. Once you know your shape you can start dressing it and showing off your shopping skills.

I tend to shop so that my overall look has a celebrity feel, but I'm buying on a budget. I like to mix stores so that my bodycon may be a bargain but my bag is Balenciaga. Whether it's hiding the Penneys price tag whilst carrying your essentials in a chic tote you saved up for, or wearing head to toe high street with those stunning designer sunglasses you begged for at Christmas, you can always create the illusion of sophistication. Working with a plain palette works really well here; dressing head to toe in black and adding a statement accessory, whether it's killer heels or an embellished neck piece, instantly ups your game. This sort of get up is classy and simplistic with a twist and means you only have to spend on the statement piece. Similarly, dressing up a plain t-shirt and jeans with a statement coat can take a drab and dreary outfit up a notch, immediately reinventing your style. The opposite also applies when you're wearing a dressy outfit; dressing it down by wearing a pair of trainers works really well and this style is worn by so many models, whether they're heading to the airport or running errands. Learning to make multiple uses out of items is another handy trick. If you invest in a scarf for example, learn how to wear it in a myriad of ways. From around your neck to draped around your shoulders or gathered in at the waist with a belt. Remember, less is more. Sometimes the more you try to look like you have money and a wonderful wardrobe the more tacky and cheap you look.

Clashing prints and labels can be fun, but trying too hard can make you look like you raided a knock off stall. Keep this in mind when it comes to accessories too. If you're wearing a little black dress and want to take it up a notch, don't go overboard adding a chunky necklace, massive cuff, bright bag and towering heels. Simplicity is key. Whatever you wear, wear it with confidence. Celebrities have a dynamic air about them and can generally pull off anything once it's styled correctly, so the brand doesn't really matter, it's the overall illusion and effect. Sticking to one colour but varying texture adds dimension, texture and interest to an otherwise plain palette. If black is too boring, you can apply this to all white, all beige, or all grey for a more funky feel. Adding an oversized floppy hat to a plain maxi dress instantly adds drama and elevates your outfit to a more stylish level. If you're not a fan of oversized statement accessories then a really nice way to add understated elegance is to layer delicate dainty pieces like gold necklaces or stackable bracelets. Sticking to the basics and adding accents is one of my favourite ways to dress from day to day. Investing in key pieces like a little black dress, a great pair of jeans, crisp shirt and leather jacket will make outfit planning a much easier task.

Highstreet Havens

There are so many amazing retail outlets out there to explore, so if designer labels are only in your dreams for the moment, get to know your go-to stores for bargain buys.

If I were to shop in one store forever it would have to be Zara. Their prices are affordable enough for most budgets and their selection is classy and elegant. From brilliant basics to dreamy dresses, hot handbags and sexy shoes I never leave there empty-handed.

TopShop and River Island come close seconds with great sale sections and on-trend pieces. H&M is handy for copying trends without the spend and has lots of really cute accessories and gym gear. Penneys is undoubtedly my most frequented store. Like most Irish women, I simply cannot leave without buying something. If I intend on buying some socks, I end up coming out with a whole winter wardrobe. Guilt-free shopping at its best, once you read the washing instructions most items last and their shoes are some of the comfiest I own. If you have a special occasion such as a wedding then French Connection and Ted Baker are my top picks. There are always gorgeous gúnas and classic garments to choose from. When it comes to high street heels, Aldo is awesome. Their selection of shoes is always stunning and is best described as catwalk meets comfort. If I'm making a splurge after saving for some time then Brown Thomas is heaven. From designer sunglasses and bags to killer heels it's my department store of choice for rare treats. Their January sale is also amazing and a great idea is to ask for vouchers at Christmas time so you can bag yourself a serious bargain.

Selecting Shapewear

In my opinion, dressing well is equally important when it comes to lingerie. The right underwear can totally transform your figure, in turn complementing your look. Ill-fitting undies can also ruin your ensemble and make you look and feel uncomfortable. So let's discuss the less aesthetic, heavy-duty options first.

As far as I'm concerned, every girl should own some sort of shapewear. Whether you have a trim and slim physique or a fuller figure, these nude knickers will smooth and shape your body into the best silhouette possible. We all have excess skin and carry more fat in certain areas. If you're more mature you may experience some sagging and want to lift your bum or tone your thighs. I used to despise Spanx. When I first invested in a pair I bought them a size too small thinking they would give my body the illusion of said size. Instead, they choked my waist, causing excess lower boob bulge and back fat. Worse still,

when I sat down in my skin-tight dress, the Spanx would roll down allowing my suffocated skin to pour out on top. I would have rathered a natural muffin top than that awkward and painful sight. What I have just described is probably something so many of us have experienced. Buying a size that's comfortable but supportive is the perfect balance. My advice is to pick a day when you have tons of time to try on various undergarment options, stand up straight, suck in, walk around and sit down to see how each item fairs.

If you simply want a streamline look without any tell-tale lines, the softer and more silky the material, the better. If you require more of a complete figure overhaul then look for material with more nylon. The harder the material, the more sucked in you'll appear, especially if there's specific compression zones that work to target generic unsightly areas, lumps or bumps. But remember, most importantly, you want to be able to breathe.

There are plenty of options to add to your shapewear selection over time. Choose from half to full shorts if you want to tone the tummy, thigh and bum area. Full body pieces give an all over lift and are ideal once concealed. There are waist trainers for a modern day comfortable corset and even bum bras if you want to create the ultimate Kim K. Play around with various styles, depending on the outfit requirements and stick to nude shades. Although white and black options are available, if it's your first time investing, nude will suit every colour in your wardrobe and washes well. In my opinion, the correct shapewear is like real life PhotoShop; it enhances every curve and tricks the eye into thinking you're at least one size smaller, so invest.

Dreamy Delicates

Now to move onto some more aesthetically pleasing undergarments. From plain and simplistic t-shirt bras and cotton briefs to intricate and dainty delicates, every girl should own some nice lingerie.

I personally adore shopping for underwear; even when I'm single I like to wear sexy pieces that make me feel feminine and well put together. We'll get to bras in a minute but let's talk pretty panties first. I'm just going to put it out there that I despise thongs. I don't like how they look or feel and I find g strings more gross than gorgeous. Don't get me wrong there are times you require no VPL; tight see through gym leggings or cotton figure hugging dresses are two examples of such occasions, but in general I avoid this style. If you're investing in a basic bikini thong try and opt for neutral colours considering they're specifically meant to be disguised. In terms of material, similar to shapewear, the more nylon and spandex the more hold and shape retention you get. Cotton briefs tend to lose their shape and become saggy after washing, which can lead to unsightly bumps. If you're after comfort then boy shorts or hipster briefs are brilliant. I tend to buy lots of different colours and prints in these so I have ample choice when it comes to decision time. I also find comfortable cotton briefs brilliant for lady time.

If you're conscious of your tummy but don't require full on shapewear then high waisted panties are perfect. I find these especially good if you're wearing a tight vest top and jeans because they hold you in just enough to shape and smooth your tummy without restricting movement or compromising comfort. If you're after something sexy then lace French knickers are always a winner. The downside is how obvious the frills are under your clothes, the upside is how amazing they make your beautiful bum look. If you're investing in lingerie for a special occasion or that special someone then go all out. From corsets to suspenders there are so many amazing options out there. Hell, investing in a bit of kink just for yourself can make you feel hot too.

Tweaking the Twins

I've always had big boobs, from the age of 13 I was wearing a 32DD bra and disliked how large they looked against my then slim, size 8 frame. Although I felt confident, my style covered my body for the most part.

My frame was top heavy until I grew into my hips and balanced out into a more hourglass shape. Over the years I've fluctuated in bra size, when I was on the contraceptive pill I reached a miserable 36G and now maintain a happy 34E. I've suffered back pain and spent more money on bras than I'd care to admit. Unfortunately, for anyone with big boobs, you need to splash that extra cash on ensuring you have adequate support to avoid sagging in the future. If you're getting fitted for the first time or returning after avoiding it for a few years, then there are a few tips I can offer.

Bra fitting can take time and involves trying on various shapes, styles and brands to see what size you are in each, so book your appointment on a day off where you have ample time, just like with your shapewear. In fact, why not designate a day to updating your underwear? Wear something loose and comfortable that's easy to take off so you won't be flustered, hot or stressed in the changing room. Getting half naked in front of a stranger can be a daunting experience, so the more comfortable you are feeling the better. If you're nervous, try and remember that your bra fitting lady does this every single day. There are no twins she hasn't tweaked, so try and relax knowing this is her job and she's not there to judge. Also, it's worth bearing in mind that

no two boobs are the same. We all have one boob slightly bigger than the other; some women have perky boobs, others sag slightly. She's seen scars and stretch marks, inverted nipples and terrific tits, so don't worry. We are all unique and different but every shape and size is beautiful. Trusting your fitter is also essential. There have been times when I've walked in with a sexy razor back bra in mind and walked out with a boring black one. What you have envisaged may not be suitable for you, and unless it's for a short occasion where you're wearing said sexy piece for visual purposes only, you need a bra that will support you and give you the best shape possible. Irrespective of your choice, be prepared to spend some money. I'm regularly tempted to purchase pieces in cheaper stores, only to watch them lose their shape after one wash.

Building Your Bra-drobe

Once you've been professionally fitted it's time to invest in some key pieces to add some perk in your lovely lumps' life. In my experience, there are five main bra types that will see you through any occasion.

The plain t-shirt bra is an essential in any collection. It's smooth and seam free, comfortable, and will sit under almost all day-to-day tops.

The strapless bra is often avoided especially for those with big boobs. I used to loath the shape strapless bras gave me; they seemed to pull my breasts down towards my waist and give a flat effect. When I came across the Wonderbra Strapless it was an instant game changer. Now one of my most-worn pieces it's perfect for strapless tops and dresses. The only bra I bring on holidays, it gives amazing lift and hand like support providing a full rounded cleavage. The thick strap means it adheres to your upper waist without slipping down and the extra clasps give great grip. Whatever strapless bra you choose be sure to look for rubber lining in the under band. This rubber lining is designed to adhere to the ribcage, preventing the bra from slipping. There's also a knack to filling these bad boys beautifully. Simply bend forward scooping your boobs into the bra whilst clasping the band at the back.

A push up bra is the addition that will take you from girl next door to Victoria's Secret model in one motion. A good push up will give you a sexy shape that's supportive and looks amazing on its own or under a simple vest top. A plunge bra is brilliant if you're looking for lift and wearing a low cut neckline. The perfect plunge will create a cleavage that's classy and the right size will ensure no overspill. A good sports bra is essential if you're running or working out. There are two types, which include encapsulating and compression. Encapsulating support sports bras are made with cups on either side to support 360 movement. Compression bras are more common, working on holding the boobs in place to prevent bouncing up and down. The wrong compression bra can give you a uni-boob. As a result, I personally find encapsulating more supportive especially for larger boobs, but once you're investing in a good brand both work well for fitness.

Boosting Your Bust

If your twins are on the smaller side, then there are lots of ways to embrace or enhance your size. I'm always jealous of girls with smaller boobs, their frame immediately looks slimmer, they can go braless, afford to spend less on lingerie and wear plunging necklines without looking tacky.

Certain jumpers also look way better on a smaller bust. When I wear a polo neck I appear immediately broader and chunky, but those with a more petite upper body look fantastic in a turtleneck. Going backless is another option I can only dream off. There's nothing sexier than showing off your back, and if you're lucky enough to be able to go braless then embrace it. Sheer and sharp shirts tend to work really well with smaller boobs too, so invest in some staples.

If you want to enhance your lady lumps then there are lots of ways to do so. As a make up artist I can tell you that the art of contour is key. By simply adding shade and highlight to certain sections, you can create the illusion of a bigger bust. Remember, the area you shade recedes and the area you highlight protrudes, so highlighting the fullest part of your bust is magic for your mounds. Then, simply add some matte bronzer to the cleavage area, scooping out the rounded shape you want to further enhance.

If make up isn't your thing then chicken fillets are your best friends. Designed to add at least half a cup size, they can be inserted into any bra or bikini to give an immediate boost. The material is specifically designed to adhere to your skin, meaning they don't move about and are virtually undetectable. If you want to add more that half a cup size than adding a chicken fillet to a padded push up bra is a winning combination. Not only does this add volume and lift but it creates that extra push. Women with a flatter chest can find it hard to fill a push up bra so adding fillets will give that extra oomph. If you're unhappy with your boobs to the point where none of the above techniques are enough then there are cosmetic options out there. I have lots of friends who have had work done, whether it's a boob reduction, lift post-pregnancy or augmentation. I'm certainly not advocating resorting to surgery, but it's good to know there's lots of choice when it comes to your body.

Shopping for Swimwear

When holiday season comes around, the impending panic begins; shopping for swimwear and getting bikini body ready can be a daunting task.

One of my favourite memes reads 'how to get bikini body ready; put a bikini on your body'. So many women panic when it comes to packing for a sunny week away because choosing the right swimwear can be a bit of a nightmare. When it comes to underwear it's hidden away for the most part and only our partner or pet sees our delicates. When you're playing by the pool or lounging on a beach there are strangers, friends and families around. There's a certain pressure that comes with having to bare all and strip down exposing our flaws to the world. I discussed body confidence in the previous chapter, but buying the right swim style to suit your shape is half the battle. Just like lingerie, there are lots of styles to choose from.

The triangle bikini is the most basic shape. I find this style suits the smaller chest best; it tends to cover the majority of the bust and has no padding. If I wear a triangle bikini I end up with six boobs and black eyes.

The halter neck bikini works really well for a bigger bust because the shape elongates the neckline, enhances the bust and gives great lift.

If you're proud of your twins but conscious of your stomach area then the high waisted bikini bottoms are your best friends. Designed to cover and shape love handles and excess folds they're a great option once you're not concerned about tan lines.

The strapless bikini is brilliant for avoiding dreaded tan lines but a really difficult one to wear. If you buy the incorrect shape the strapless bikini can turn two boobs into one flat pancake, which is most unflattering. Your best bet is to buy a bikini with a removable strap so you can wear it strapless lying down while tanning and add the strap for support and lift whilst moving.

If a two-piece is too terrifying then there are plenty of swimsuits out there. Gone are the days when the only one piece you could buy resembled something from *Fame*, there are so many stylish options to choose from now. If your tummy is your problem area then try a swimsuit with gathered material around your mid section to distract the eye away from the area you're most conscious of. Similarly if

love handles are an issue gathered material on either side works really well. The thicker the support and straps the better the boobs will look. If you're wearing a one piece you can make it slightly sexier by ensuring your boobs are perky and full, giving an overall flattering look. If you're on holidays at lots of pool parties, one pieces also look great paired with cut off shorts for a funky look that's more covered up than dancing in your two piece.

Be Adventurous With Your Attire

So now that we've covered most fashion fixes from flattering your figure, dressing for less and battling with booby traps the best advise I can give you is to have fun. Visit a store you would never usually go into, browse bargains in the sale rails and start stocking up on staples.

Classy casual clothes speak for themselves and dresses that take you from day to night make updating your style less of a hassle. Being savvy when you shop can save you time and effort. For example saving up for an item you know is timeless vs. splurging on a temporary trend you'll hate within a year or two. Being assertive when choosing your attire is a great habit to get into; asking yourself key questions before you hand over you money can really pay off in the long run. Will you get wear out of that sparkly playsuit, or is it a once off? Will that leather jacket last until next season? I tend to save my money for big pieces that are classic colours, amazing quality and go with at least three items in my wardrobe. That way, when I want to try out a trend I'm fond of I can shop around and find it on the highstreet, and avoid feeling guilty if I only wear it once or dislike it a year on. The likes of an LBD can be worn in so many different ways so why not allocate more money on it? I used to be a magpie for sequins and unique items, only to leave them collecting dust on the rail because they never paired well with anything. A black dress may seem like a simplistic and boring spend, but trust me it's worth it. You can accessories it with dainty jewellery and scrappy heels for a dinner date, add a statement piece and clutch for a club night, pair it with a blazer for the office or dress it down with grunge boots and a biker jacket. Whatever you wear, wear it with confidence and a smile to suit your style.

Chapter **8**

Fairy
Fitness

Junk Food Journey

My relationship with food has been a bit of a rollercoaster over the years. Luckily I've never suffered from an eating disorder per se, but I've been an extremist with my eating habits.

I was a very healthy child; I opted for hot pink radishes over sweets, I ate ample amounts of fruit and veg and we never bought fizzy drinks or crisps in our household. Our treat meal was a burger and chips from the local chipper on a Friday evening after horse riding and we otherwise avoided fast food.

As I matured and began to make my own food choices things changed. Looking back, I had the ability to eat large quantities without gaining weight; even when I had a sandwich with my main meal or a full packet of cheese strings. I was tall and slim with a good metabolism similar to my mum. When I was old enough to party and drink I began to eat more fast food, crisps, chocolate, and fizzy drinks. Take aways were more frequent than home-cooked meals and I was exercising less. I gave up most of the sports I had enjoyed in my younger years including ballet, gymnastics, hockey and athletics.

As I moved into my twenties, my frame expanded into an hourglass shape and my poor diet began affecting my skin and energy levels. I don't think I realised I was binging on heavy foods because I felt I had a normal relationship with food. I ate when I was happy and when I was sad. I didn't emotionally eat, I just kept eating without thinking about what I was putting into my body and how I was going to expend the extra calories. I ate when I was bored and when I wasn't actually hungry. I suppose having had a naturally slim frame throughout my teens, I continued the mindset of being able to eat what I wanted without getting fat which is nonsensical to say the least. The more drink I consumed on a night out, the worse I ate the following day. When Monday morning came around I began feeling guilty about my gorge over the weekend and I would start a 'diet'. I didn't buy diet books or pills, I just devised my own eating plan based on my collation of ill-educated knowledge of what I considered bad and good foods.

Vicious Cycle

If I wanted to drop a few pounds, carbs were bad and water was good.

If I had to squeeze into a size 12 dress, I would have Special K for breakfast, tuna and popcorn for lunch and a mocha or more Special K for dinner. I was burning the candle at both ends working long shifts and partying hard. I was miserable, tired, grumpy and hungry from Monday to Friday, and ecstatic when Saturday came around when I could eat all the food and drink all the drink. This cycle continued for a few years and wreaked havoc on my relationship with food and my body. Instead of losing weight, I gained more and I began to feel down about the way I looked, and more importantly about the way I felt.

Finally, at the age of 27, I decided to completely overhaul my lifestyle. I educated myself on food, the food groups I needed, how much I required and when. I went through stints of following a healthy diet and fitness regime but fell off the bandwagon every now and then. It was only after a big break up that I decided to make the change for good and find a balance that would last a lifetime. I began to realise the benefits of certain produce and the negative effects of others. I started to treat my body like a machine that I needed to fuel and ate for the purpose of living healthily, as opposed to wanting to stuff my face or needing to zip up that smaller size. The first few weeks were the hardest; I was either hungry and craving the bad foods I was used to consuming or full from bland bites. I had the usual worries that weight training while I carried extra fat would make me bulky. After about a month of sticking with my changes, my skin became more clear, my energy levels soared, my sleep pattern improved, my anxiety was reduced and I was losing pounds, inches and body fat. For the first time in my adult life I was living a life I had complete control over, I no longer simply strived for a successful career, I was working towards a successful body too. I treated my new shape like my home, kept it tidy and maintained it well, instead of just expecting it to look after itself. Just like a mortgage, I was thinking long term and putting efforts and payments down now to reap the benefits later.

Cheating Clean

A really important element of any lifestyle change is ensuring it's easily maintained. The reason why diets don't work in general is simply because they restrict important food groups or involve meal planning options that can lead to a decrease in energy, and increase in headaches, hunger pangs and junk food cravings.

Sure, you drop weight on the scales quickly initially, but what damage is it doing to your metabolism long term, and is it worth the horrific side effects?

The important thing that so many people forget about when they get excited by swift weight loss is how it's impossible to maintain. Most women, especially during certain times of the month, suffer from cravings, so banning treats altogether and being too regimented in short bursts can wreak havoc on your system. As soon as you start to indulge in said foods again, your body will store them as fat, or worse, you'll be inclined to binge eat and stuff your face with all of the things you have been obsessing about, only to feel immediately guilty afterwards. Trust me I've been there. I've been scared of carbs and cut them so low that my mood was affected, my concentration was poor, I was constantly lethargic, I lost strength during weight training in turn losing muscle and definition and I was hungry all the time. I was borderline ketosis, a condition characterised by raised levels of ketones in the body, associated with abnormal fat metabolism and diabetes mellitus.

As soon as I reintroduced carbs into my diet all of these side effects were gone, I felt happier and healthier and in turn more in control of my choices. I started to learn to appreciate the fact that carbs gave me energy, when I needed it, and how protein would repair my muscles. I also learned ways to curb cravings without over-indulging. The detrimental cycle of dieting, binging, gaining weight and dieting is vicious and so easy to fall into, even if you don't suffer from an eating disorder. Most magazines have headlines that help you lose 7lbs in one week or comment on celebrity body shapes and changes, which can unconsciously affect our way of thinking. We are bombarded with perfected body images on TV, in print and now splashed all over social media. All you have to do is look up hashtags, scroll the feed and feel instantly insecure about your own body. Focusing on what works for you and your attainable body goals is integral. Balance is also key if you want slow, steady results that last a lifetime. If you spend your time focusing on imitating what other people are doing for their body shape, you remain stagnant. Having a guideline goal is great, but expecting your body to react the same as someone with completely different genetic make up, frame and fitness routine is deluded.

Taking Baby Steps

Sometimes starting off is the trickiest task; the end goal seems so far away, new foods are foreign, exercise is gruelling and you can become overwhelmed by all of the contradictory advice out there.

Simple, gradual changes to your mind set and food choices have a far greater overall effect than you may think. I used to skip breakfast in the morning or reach for full fat milk and a sugary cereal that would cause my energy levels to crash by 11am. Switching my cereal for oats and my milk for unsweetened almond milk now means I'm satisfied, full of slow release energy and guilt-free until lunch. I love adding berries to my oats and if I'm training I also add some protein powder. This means I get extra protein throughout the day to repair my muscles, the flavour of whey adds to my oats making them tastier and the consistency changes overall to taste more like a treat.

At the weekend, when I once craved a greasy fry, I now have an omelette packed with greens, turkey sausages, chicken or chorizo, and low fat feta instead of full fat cheddar cheese. This alternative meal is far more satisfying and still feels like a cheat.

Gone are the college days when I reached for a large bread roll filled with mayo, chicken fillet and cheese with a side of crisps and chocolate washed down with a bottle of coke for my lunch. I now have a protein or gluten free wrap with greens, tuna or chicken mix and rice or corn cakes with tasty toppings and lots of water. Instead of feeling stuffed, lacking concentration and feeling tired from my food coma, I'm perfectly full, filled with energy and happiness from my positive choices.

At dinner I used to eat late, order take aways at home or eat a three course meal on a night out. Now I have chicken or fish with rice, or sweet potatoes with a dessert of peanut butter and some apple slices or rice cakes and Nutella. That's right I said Nutella; I'm addicted to the glorious jar of hazelnut goodness and I allow myself a spoonful a day. Instead of gorging on bars of chocolate or biscuits mindlessly I allocate a treat a day, whether it's a spoonful of spread or two squares of dark chocolate. When emotion is attached to food choices and you're told you can't have certain items you'll think about them more than average and tend to over eat when you break the ban. I simply change my treat of choice so that it's a slightly healthier option, taken in moderation and I don't feel deprived.

Meal Planning

One of my most highly requested blog posts that has received thousands of hits has been a meal plan for women. Considering I'm not a nutritionist or a personal trainer I must point out the following sample diet is a rough guide to my daily diet devised with my trainer.

Everyone is different, we all have different genetics, metabolism, weight, height, goals, likes and dislikes so please feel free to tailor this plan to suit you and treat it like a sample guide. The idea behind the plan was to eat six small meals a day so that I would feel full, get all of the nutrients I required and allow enough cheats that I could stick to it and not stray.

The following meal plan is primarily aimed at those who currently have no structured eating plan through the week and eat what is most readily available to them. It's designed to help decrease body fat and help in the building of lean muscle throughout the body when combined with a regular resistance training programme. This combination has worked for me and can be effective for most women who want similar results. It's also to improve overall health by avoiding foods that may be detrimental. By having a structured meal plan for each day people tend to find it easier to avoid foods that will cause them to gain weight and more importantly, body fat, which I'll discuss shortly.

With a more structured plan like the one below, that has more regular eating times, higher protein throughout the diet, and more varied carbohydrates and fats, cleaner eating and more sustainable fat loss results can be achieved. If I'm away or on holidays I don't stick strictly this plan; I eat out, I order what I want without feeling guilty but my daily diet goes something like this. Again, balance is key here and it's nice to have a blow out every now and then but return to structure.

	MONDAY	TUESDAY	WEDNESDAY	THURSDAY	FRIDAY	SATURDAY	SUNDAY
Meal 1	Eggs, wholegrain toast, 2 slices of watermelon	Porridge, protein powder and blueberries	Fruit salad, chopped apple, strawberry, pineapple and mixed berries	Protein pancakes from day before	Eggs, wholegrain toast, strawberries	Omelette with meat and veg of your choice	Scrambled egg on wholegrain brown bread
Meal 2	Protein shake and banana pre-workout for energy	Fruit salad, chopped apple, strawberry, pineapple and mixed berries	Protein pancakes, topped with almonds and fruit	Protein shake and banana pre-workout for energy	Peanut butter rice cakes with flaked almonds	Fruit salad	Apple and peanut butter
Meal 3	Protein shake, 2 rice cakes with peanut butter for post-workout recovery	Chicken salad from night before	Salmon fillet, boiled eggs, pasta	Greek yoghurt with granola	Beef lettuce cups, ground beef wrapped in a large lettuce leaf	Small bowl of porridge	Roast chicken, sweet potato, broccoli and carrots
Meal 4	2 chicken fillets, wholegrain rice and green beans	Protein shake or bar, choice of nuts and/or seeds to snack on	Greek yoghurt with granola	Tuna salad, light mayo, sweetcorn, lettuce, peppers, cucumber and onion	Wholegrain bagel with turkey, mixed leaves, and avocado	Protein wrap with chicken and feta salad	Mixed nuts, cashews, hazelnuts, almonds, etc.
Meal 5	Greek yoghurt, blueberries and a spoonful of honey	Beef, sweet potato and broccoli. Beef can be handmade into burgers	Fish fillets with homemade coleslaw and mixed salad	Protein smoothie, blended natural yoghurt, mixed fruits and protein powder	Protein bar	Cheat meal	Homemade beef lasagne
Meal 6	Chicken, spinach, chopped mixed peppers, lettuce and cashew nuts	Small snack of peanut butter rice cakes if needed to fill a gap	Flapjacks, sunflower seeds, poppy seeds, oats, flax seeds and honey	Turkey mince, peppers, onions and sweet potato fries	Chicken stir fry with mixed vegetables and noodles	(Optional) something low calorie post-cheat meal	Strawberry greek yoghurt

My **TOP 10** Clean Treats

I've obviously tweaked my meal plan over time, finding new additions and tricks to add flavour to otherwise plain portions. I've put together my top ten 'cheat clean' items that should make your food shop a little bit more exciting. Most of the items below, aside from regular supermarket stock, can be found online from www.boyfirstnutrition.ie or from their Dublin stores in Clontarf and Malahide.

Turkey Sausages and Mince
These are two meat additions I regularly reach for. In the morning I can cook the sausages in coconut oil for a guilt free fry, chop them up and add them to an omelette at lunch or add them to rice for dinner. Turkey mince is brilliant for mixing with peppers, onions and seasoning to add to rice or lettuce cups.

P28 Protein Wraps
These are one of my favourite discoveries. White bread was my weakness when I first started this lifestyle change and I was constantly on the hunt for an alternative. These wraps are excellent for people who are trying to build muscle and lose body fat.

Cheeses **Goat's Cheese** and **feta** are
both high in protein and calcium, low in fat and sodium and a brilliant cheddar alternative. My two favourite cheeses of choice, I add them to salads, on spelt crackers, melted in rice or omelettes, and with meat.

Wheyhey
This is another protein-packed discovery that changed my movie nights forever. The world's first protein ice cream. Say goodbye to Ben & Jerry and hey to this whey alternative. The chocolate tub is terrific.

Dr. Karg Spelt Crackers
These crackers have made my lunch time more exciting. Made with spelt, the grain that's packed with complex carbohydrates and high in protein, they come with a variety of topping options like sesame and sunflower seeds or tomato and mozzarella flavouring. These are delicious topped with chicken or turkey slices, spinach, rocket and low fat cream cheese as an ideal sandwich alternative.

Tesco Light Mayo
This has the best nutritional value I've found and the nicest flavour. I find most meat quite dry if eaten daily so I like to add a small amount of mayo to mix with tuna or chicken.

Frank's Red Hot Sauce
This has no nutritional value, but it also has no calories either and tastes great. I add it to scrambled eggs, over salads, mixed with tuna and mayo, add it to meat mixes and basically anything I want full of flavour. If you like restaurant-style buffalo wings then this will become your best friend.

Nutramino Protein Bars
These are probably my favourite fitness find of all time. If you're a fan of Bounty, Snickers, Mars or Moro bars, then be prepared to fall in love with these babies and never look back. By far my Holy Grail, protein bar of choice I always have these with me on the go for emergencies and when I want something sweet as a treat.

Emily Fruit Crisps
These are a super snack to bring with you travelling or on a cinema date when you're avoiding the snack stand. They're also a terrific topping for yoghurt and an excellent ingredient for home baking.

Low Cal Jelly
This is a must for those with a sweet tooth. If the above meal plan and sweet treats leave you longing for more then this treat is ideal with many brands being just 10 calories per pot.

Super Supplements

If your diet is on point then there's very little supplementary additions you'll need bar the odd vitamin or drink to fuel your fitness if you're training intensely.

I like to take some Stress B, which are great during my period as they help with alertness, protect my immune system and help my mood.

I also take Omega Fish Oils for their mental health benefits and fat burning and muscle building aid.

There are also three training supplements I like to use that work really well together but aren't essential.

Prior to training I didn't even drink coffee, so caffeine somewhat scared me. Bodyfirst Nutrition went through my options with me and educated me on the various effects caffeine could have. I discovered that a pre-workout drink before intense training sessions such as a heavy leg day or having caffeine when you need that extra boost of energy and strength is brilliant.

My energy drink of choice is FKD, which works really well, tastes like cola and has no nasty side effects.

Intra workouts are also a nice addition or alternative to pre-workout supplements. ON Essential Amino Energy has natural energisers, Beta Alanine, and boosting ingredients to help you reach your next level and at just 10 calories per serving it's a tasty drink option for during your workout.

If you decide against pre and intra workout supplements, a post-workout protein shake is a staple in any training regime. I generally buy a different flavour each time so I don't tire of the taste. I use protein powder in my oats, to make protein pancakes or balls and to use as a shake post-training. I love the Optimum Nutrition Whey Protein in Cookies & Cream and Mint Chocolate.

Counting Macros

There are lots of ways to track your food when you first embark on a lifestyle change. You can keep a hand written food diary, fill in a food table on your computer or use a phone app.

I personally prefer the latter as it's so convenient and easy to stick with. Tracking your food isn't a necessity, but I find it really helps to keep you focused. MyFitnessPal is an app that's tailored to your body and goals and has weigh in options, a food and exercise diary and progress charts. The app is free so there's no excuse not to at least download it and give it a try. I'm quite obsessive compulsive when it comes to note-taking and I worried it would be another unnecessary addition

to my workload and task I would have to maintain but it's so easy to keep on top of. There's a bar code scanner that remembers your favourite foods and their nutritional values or you can manually enter them yourself. You can compile regularly eaten meals and recipes which means adding your daily food intake is a breeze. The app manually subtracts the calories burned when you enter exercise that you have done.

When I went on diets in the past I always looked at the caloric value of food instead of the broken down nutrition. Put simply, there are three macronutrients: proteins, fats and carbs. Protein helps to build and repair

muscle. Fat is required for brain functionality, hormone regulation and much more. Carbs are our main energy source and the most commonly cut macro in most ill-informed diets.

After entering your information, MyFitnessPal will advise you on what macros you should be hitting everyday and help you track them. Instead of worrying about calories or cutting certain food groups, counting macros means you can eat more or less what you want once you're staying within your advised grams and eating good food in moderation. Also known as 'If It Fits Your Macros', this is an increasingly popular way to 'diet' in a positive and pleasurable way.

Step Away From the Scales

When you commence a new relationship with food and exercise it can be tempting to use a weighing scales as a milestone marker. A weigh in every few months is fine, but I would highly advise removing the scales from your house because your weight is not an indication of health or progress as such.

Every month or so I get my trainer to measure my body fat using a callipers and record my inch loss using a measuring tape. Although body fat testing isn't always 100% accurate, once you have the same trainer measure you each time and the results are decreasing in a slow and steady manner, you can judge your development. These two methods are great ways to keep track of your progress and not lose sight of your goals.

When I started my journey, my body fat was 30%, which is above average for a woman. I'm now at a healthy 24% and have lost inches overall, which match my dress size decrease. I'm actually only a stone and a half down on the scales but I've gained muscle through heavy weight lifting, so I try to ignore that number altogether. During my period I often gain up to 6lbs of water weight, which again can really affect your mindset when you're eating well and working hard in the gym. Invest more time in how you look and feel as you move on in your journey and avoid trying to rush a process that's intended for life. Fad diets will get your weight down on the scales for a few weeks but will never stand the test of time. Slow and steady weight loss and muscle gain can take a couple of years but you'll never revert back to your old ways so it's worth your while being positive and patient.

Fit Fashion

Investing in fit fashion is something I used to despise prior to my transformation. I spent all my money on dresses for nights out and popped on the same black leggings and vest top for the very rare occasion I decided to workout in the form of a Zumba or Pilates class.

Considering I didn't even have a gym membership at the time, I didn't care for spending money on sportswear. Now, my daily dress code is gym gear, in fact I probably own more gym gear than night out dresses now and my wash basket is 95% exercise attire. I get more excited about a new pair of neon leggings than I do about a pair of jeans. Since changing my outlook on fitness and sticking to my routine, working out is a huge part of my week and as a result I've invested in some staples that make me feel bright and bubbly heading to the gym. My theory is that if you feel gorgeous in what you wear on the outside you'll feel better on the inside, which can in turn aid your training. If you wear the right gym gear you'll focus on the task at hand, perform better and feel more at ease with how you look in those horrific floor to ceiling magnified mirrors.

I personally adore clashing colours, pretty patterns and matching my ensemble to my runners. I think you can afford to spend less on items like coloured crops, vests and runners for days when you'll be focusing on areas such as upper body but you need to spend more on items like sports bras, leggings that will retain their shape and good supportive runners for cardio classes and high impact training. Whatever your budget, fitness fashion should be fun and help motivate you to hit the gym.

Exercise

I was never a lazy person in that I always kept busy career, hobby and social life wise, but I was completely demotivated when it came to exercise.

I was that girl who relied on genetics but gradually put on weight through poor diet and lack of fitness and just hoped I would stay a similar shape. I was allergic to the gym, found classes boring, assumed weights made you masculine and thought cardio was only running on a treadmill. Until I decided to join a gym, get a personal trainer and educate myself on the options available in terms of working out. I no longer wanted a quick fix, I truly wanted to change, wanted to lose weight, and wanted to tone up, I wanted to challenge myself and I wanted to be healthy.

My WEEKLY Workout

Monday – Spin HIIT

Tuesday – Legs & Shoulders

Wednesday – Circuits &/or Kettlebells

Thursday – Back & Biceps

Friday – Chest & Triceps

Sunday – Body Attack & CX Works

After my first consultation I was given a personal programme and a run through of the classes available and what they were good for. I was also shown all of the equipment available and how to use each machine. I wanted a varied routine so I wouldn't bore of my timetable and ensured a different daily challenge. I progressed from being out of breath, with a red sweaty face after five minutes of high intensity training to now enduring 45 minutes to two hour training sessions. I've increased my strength and ability dramatically, advanced on machines I was scared of, feel confident working out alone or with friends and most importantly I've learned to love exercise. Not only has it changed my body for the better, it's the only time in my day that I completely switch off from every personal stress and work worry. Just like my diet, my workout routine is tailored to my body, ability and goals. It's also a rough example; some weeks change depending on my schedule and progress. However, I've worked alongside my trainer to suggest the top five exercises in each category to suit the majority of women embarking on a weight lifting and cardio incorporated programme.

For women to grow lean muscle there are specific exercises that are particularly beneficial for the growth of lean muscle to tone and shape the body. The exercises are classified into different muscle groups: legs, chest, back, shoulders, biceps and triceps. This is why it's advised to do muscle group specific days as you can see by my sample week above. All of the exercises I have included can be done in a gym with the appropriate machines. If you don't have a PT to show you each exercise then I would advise looking up each one on YouTube to ensure you're carrying them out effectively.

Legs

*When training your **legs** it's important to train all parts of them including quads, glutes, hamstrings and calves.*

My number one exercise for developing the quads and glutes is the squat. The squat requires stability, coordination, good core strength and is fantastic for loading the legs with heavy weight to build lean muscle.

To develop the glutes, the weighted step up is one of my favourite exercises to do. Keeping one foot on a step, while bringing your other knee to a 90° angle, this move will keep the glutes activated and help to improve stability and balance.

To develop the quads the leg extension will help to bring out more definition. For hamstrings, the stiff leg deadlift is one that is hard to perform initially but when practised enough the benefits are worth the time spent mastering the move. It builds lean muscle, can target specific parts of the hamstring by changing stance and improves the strength of the lower back. To train the calves, a calf raise machine with very high repetitions is going to be one of the easiest ways to develop the definition of the calves without adding size to them.

Back

*For developing the **back** it's important to make sure that all of the muscles in the back are worked and not just the parts that women can sometimes be most concerned with, which are those that are most visible.*

To make sure to hit all the muscles in the back it's important to hit variations of rows and pulldowns. The wide grip lat pulldown and underhand lat pulldown will help with this. Along with these exercises it's important to make sure the lower back stays as strong as those muscles through the mid and upper back. To do this it's best to train it similarly to the calf with high reps to build endurance and definition.

Chest

The chest can be separated into lower, middle, upper and inner and outer chest.

The upper chest can targeted with a move such as the incline barbell and dumbbell press. Ideally performed at a 45 degree angle on a bench to make sure the shoulders aren't over used in the move. The lower and middle chest can be targeted by the same moves simply by changing the angle of the exercise to a flat bench or decline bench move. To target the inner chest, a narrow grip on all presses will help and to stretch the chest. This can be done on machines, cables or with dumbbells but should be done with light weights.

Shoulders

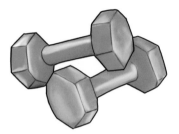

*The **shoulders** are often worked well through the moves done training the chest and back. Chest exercises will work the front of the shoulder and back exercises will train the back of the shoulders.*

The barbell and dumbbell press will build muscle well through the outer shoulder and can be done in a seated or standing position. This will be a particularly heavy weight exercise in comparison to a lot of other shoulder exercises. Lateral and front raises will be light weight exercises done with higher reps and will be good for bringing out each part of the shoulder individually. The upright row is again another heavier weight exercise ideal for building up muscle.

Biceps & Triceps

*The last areas to be hit would be the arms, which are the **biceps** and more particularly for women the **triceps** which are the back of the arms most women dislike.*

Both of these muscles will be used throughout all of the other upper body exercises but can still be used further in isolated exercises. As both of the muscles will be used so much during back and chest exercises it's best to just hit these muscles with short and effective exercises. For the biceps, preacher curls, hammer curls and standing barbell curls will target all areas of the biceps. For hitting the triceps effectively it is best to use three different variations of moves again. The French press or more commonly known as the skull crusher, the overhead cable, barbell or dumbbell extension and a cable tricep push down. These moves will effectively help build strength and tone and shape the arms.

When it comes to making a better body for yourself, it's important to keep building lean muscle through your weight training exercises but also to keep improving your fitness and burning excess body fat. High intensity interval training is the best way of achieving both and can be very difficult to do in the gym by yourself so if you feel it's not manageable or enjoyable to do by yourself, classes may be your best bet. As you can see by my weekly workout I try and incorporate my

favourite HIIT classes, which include Spin HIIT, Circuits, Kettlebells, and Body Attack by Les Mills. By using all of the above suggestions to the best of your ability your results should come in steadily and be easier to maintain than results that are achieved through diet alone.

Maintaining Motivation

An important disclaimer throughout this entire chapter is the fact that I'm not a professional or an expert on fitness by any means.

I'm just an average girl who successfully overhauled her health, mind and body for the better. I don't promote fad diets, I don't believe in quick fixes and I've worked really hard to make small changes in my appearance and ever bigger ones in my mindset. I have a curvy frame and broad build, I admire all shapes and sizes and believe everyone should simply be the best that they can be, do what makes them happy and remove the things that don't. If your weight is bothering you, my advice would be to do something about it today. It's so easy to think about that instant gratification and forget about the long-term plan and goal. Ordering that take away now may satisfy an immediate craving but it won't benefit you or your wallet in any way, shape or form and you'll probably regret it long term. Everything in moderation is important, so when you do decide to have a cheat or treat make sure you enjoy it, guilt free.

I constantly get mails from girls asking how I stay motivated. The truth is you have to really want to change with every inch of your marrow. My waking thought is what to eat, so I have found ways to continue to love food but treat it differently. I had to change my opinion of exercise and push myself and change my mindset in order to love it. There are plenty of days I'm too down or tired to go to the gym but I go anyway. Sometimes I have to switch my mind off, drive there and once I'm in the building I actually want to workout. After working out I always feel amazing, I feel accomplished and ready to take on the rest of the day and have never, ever regretted a workout. I save images of body shapes I admire, I screenshot recipes of healthy food I want to try, I keep a mood diary that records how I feel which in turn links to food and fitness. As bizarre as it sounds, if I've eaten well all day and feel falsely hungry I try on lingerie or swimwear to stay on track and avoid eating crap. I keep myself busy because I know I'm not really hungry when I'm bored and I workout when I'm happy or sad so that emotion doesn't take over my drive. Take your time, accept your genetics and work with what you have, learn to embrace your big bum or tone your thick thighs, carve and sculpt your slim shoulders or bring out your beautiful back muscles. We are all beautiful and can only do our best so don't be too hard on yourself either.

Chapter **9**

Beauty
Buzz

Beauty and Blunders

I've been immersed in the beauty industry for the past 8 years and as a result I have trialled almost every brand out there.

Working as a make up artist and model I've learned to conceal blemishes and put together some of my favourite beauty buys to create unique looks. I've tested treatments, revamped my own skin care regime, blogged about the latest technologies and ingredients, and found the perfect facial formulation. I've also experienced my own beauty blunders, from unsightly spots to stretch marks and even allergic reactions that really knocked my confidence. From cliché to clear skin, beauty really is about learning to love yourself from the inside out, from bad moods to blemishes. There are so many flaw fixers out there that can help ease ailments and make you look good on the outside and in turn improve your self-confidence.

In terms of my skin story, I've been lucky enough with my genetic make up for the most part. I have a combination skin type that's relatively normal. I experience a certain amount of shine on my t-zone throughout the day but become dehydrated when I'm working too much on the computer or lacking sleep. I've never experienced extreme issues like acne or excessively dry skin but I've had a fair few bumps in the road. When I was in college I had a nasty wasp sting, which led to an allergic reaction. After being given medication to reduce the swelling I became extremely sensitive. My skin changed dramatically leading to dry sore patches that resembled eczema for a few months. It was at this turning point that I realised I had really taken my skin for granted. Unable to wear make up, I searched the internet for the best creams to soothe and stabilise my skin again. After a sun holiday the dry patches cleared up and I promised to value and look after my skin from that moment on. Even after various GP visits, using steroidal creams and other online suggestions the sun was the only thing that really helped.

Finding Your Skin Type

There are four main skin types which can be looked after differently. Normal skin types tend to have very few, if any, imperfections. The skin is balanced, pores go unnoticed, there's no sensitivity and it generally appears radiant regardless of diet or skincare.

Combination skin types can be normal or dry in some areas and oily in others, namely the nose, forehead and chin, otherwise known as the t-zone. Combination skin is the most common skin type and can show varying attributes. The oily parts of the skin can show visible pores and blackheads, excess sebum and shine. The drier areas can be rough or flakey or normal depending on the individual.

Oily skin types tend to be shiny all the time, require mattifying products and skincare that reduces the excess sebum production. Sebum can cause blackheads that turn into blemishes and enlarged pores that turn into pimples. Puberty, hormonal imbalances and the weather can exacerbate this skin type.

Dry skin types can be the most difficult to deal with. Sometimes sensitive they can crack, peel, become itchy, irritated and inflamed. A dull, rough skin type, it has less elasticity and therefore shows signs of ageing like fine lines and wrinkles. Although pores are virtually invisible, dry skin can have patchy red areas instead.

My Skincare Routine

Throughout my teenage years I used make up wipes to remove my make up. Aside from SPF creams on holidays, they were the only skincare effort I made.

I'm now surprised that I got away with using wipes for so long, considering they simply strip your skin and offer no beauty benefits whatsoever.

Although I spent time on my make up application, I was lazy when it came to cleansing. After an informative year in beauty college, I discarded my wipes and developed a regime that contained at least 7 more steps. I now cleanse, tone, use a serum and eye cream, day and night creams, exfoliate and use a mask weekly. I know the importance of looking after your skin now in order to prevent ageing at a later stage. I also know what a difference it makes to my make up if I'm freshly exfoliated and hydrated. There really is no point in spending hundreds of euros on new make up items if your skincare is lacking. No matter how tired I am after a long day or how late it is after a night out, I no longer resort to reaching for a pack of wipes. There are so many micellar water options available now that pre-cleanse the skin and offer a quick and convenient option so there really is no excuse not to do it properly.

One of my favourite things to do is an at home facial, which consists of removing my make up with a pre-cleanse, cleansing my skin a second time with a facial brush and foaming cream, removing dead skin cells using a scrub, applying a purifying mask to clogged areas and applying a moisturising mask to dry patches. I follow up with a toner, eye cream, serum and night cream to really feel pampered. There's something so nice about allocating at least ten minutes of your night to looking after yourself. An at home facial is the perfect way to unwind and treat yourself to something that will pay off in the long run. Although I've found some bargain beauty buys in the past, I tend to stick to high-end items when it comes to my skin.

My TOP 5 SKINCARE PRODUCTS

The **Clarsonic Mia Sonic Skin Cleansing System** quite literally changed my skin for the better within a week and has remained at my sink ever since. This convenient facial brush features two speeds and is suitable for all skin types, making taking your make up off a fun task. The idea behind a facial brush of this kind is to cleanse six times more effectively than hands alone. This tool works terrifically with a foaming cleanser so I like to pair it with Origins Checks & Balances, which is a gentle, frothy face wash that doesn't strip the skin or leave it feeling tight.

Kiehl's Daily Reviving Concentrate launched recently and I began raving about it on social media after three days of use. This serum contains a blend of 100% natural origin ingredients including ginger root essential oils, tamanu and sunflower seed botanical oils. The formula smells divine, is lightweight, quickly absorbed and helps strengthen and protect the skin barrier for a smooth, fresh and healthy look all day long.

Image The Max is my go-to day and night eye cream, which contains growth factors derived from plant stem cells to protect skin cells and prevent ageing effects. If you want parabon-free protection then this reduces the appearance of fine lines, wrinkles and puffiness.

Lancôme Visionnaire is my favourite luxurious moisturiser, made with a combination of LR 2412 and hyaluronic acid, this ultra sensorial cream has a fabulous fresh yet hydrating texture. Lightweight and cooling upon application, this gorgeous gloop glides across your skin leaving it silky smooth. Unlike most lightweight creams that have a gel-like consistency, this gives heavy duty hydration. After only a few uses I was hooked, which rarely happens me so early on in testing a new product.

Glamglow are by far my Holy Grail magic masks. Their best-selling Youthmud is suitable for any skin type looking for a noticeable 3 day glow and offers brighter more radiant, soft and smooth skin in minutes. This resurfacing exfoliator penetrates into the deepest layers of the skin to tighten, tone and lift the skin. If you're concerned about dark circle, pores, or impurities this is a miracle worker.

My Hair

I wasn't blessed with good hair, in fact it's always been a concern of mine. So many people think I have gorgeous, long, luscious locks but that's down to good styling, great products and extensions.

Although my hair was thick and shiny when I was a child, I regularly dyed it in my teenage years, causing lots of hair stress and damage.

My hair suffered massively after an operation I had at the age of 18. I had endured recurring throat infections and had regular antibiotics in a bid to clear them until the point when I was forced to have my tonsils taken out at a somewhat late stage. The operation and health strain caused my hair to fall out and become weak and fine. I didn't lose my hair in chunks or have bald patches, instead it just gradually became thinner, lost volume and fell flat on my head. If I used heated tools on it to curl or straighten it would break, and dye was an absolute no go. The texture and appearance of my hair changed so dramatically that I began researching ways to help this situation that was affecting my confidence massively.

Having good hair is something every girl wants and when your hair starts to deteriorate it can really get you down. It's a sign of femininity, something to style and should add to your look, not take away from it. I remember crying over pictures of my younger self's hair, wishing it was the same and wondering how I could work on things to get it back. Aside from supplements that would help nourish from the inside I wanted a superficial way to temporality thicken my hair, and extensions seemed to be the obvious answer. Over the years I tried every extension under the sun from clip in wefts to keratin bonds, ponytails, the lot. It was only about three years ago when I was introduced to Easilocks that I found a solution and I've never looked back.

Lock Love

Unlike other methods out there, Easilocks is a system that requires no heat, no glue, no sewing or braiding and as a result cause no stress or damage to your natural hair.

By virtue of the fact that my hair was already under stress, the last thing I wanted to do was exacerbate the issue.

Easilocks extensions are applied using tiny beads, which are placed at the root of the hair, clamped and flattened attaching to your own hair. They look and feel just as natural as your own hair and are just as comfortable to wear. The Easilock method is the only hair extension system available that has been carefully designed to preserve the integrity of your natural hair whilst adding volume and length, without having to worry about the long-term effects. The brand ticked every box and I met with the owner to have them applied. After getting a full set I was hooked. They blend incredibly well with the natural hair, are virtually undetectable to the eye, available in a variety of sizes, lengths, colours and textures. Easilocks use only the finest 100% human remy hair carefully chosen from around the world, guaranteeing the most natural results and integrating beautifully with every hair type and texture.

In terms of longevity, Easilocks can be worn for 3 months without any servicing and the hair is reusable again and again, making this system affordable for every budget. Because I have such fine hair I try to make it to the salon every ten weeks to get a fresh set in, which avoids any damage. Three years on, my hair has never looked healthier and I can't recommend the brand enough. The boost in confidence I've had since wearing extensions can't be expressed in words. Instead of waking up to see my thin hair and worrying about what was causing it or reminding myself of how unhappy I was with how it looked, I now enjoy styling my hair, forget I have any issues and go about my day with one less thing to worry about. Things like going to the gym and taking holidays thankfully aren't an issue unlike other protein or glue bonded extensions that can

really suffer when exposed to heat and chlorine. I simply tie my hair up in a bun or plait while I work out and do the same for swimming pools if I don't want to get my hair wet.

Hair Routine

In terms of looking after my hair I like to keep my routine relatively simple and stick to products that I know work well with my extensions.

I don't mind investing money in the products I use because having used cheaper ones in the past I know that they simply don't work well with my hair type. Some girls have amazing, naturally thick and shiny hair and can use any shampoo and conditioner combo. I have naturally oily hair at the root with dry ends that require that little bit of extra attention, meaning my hair is difficult to deal with. I've experimented with hair colour in the past but tend to play around with the colour of my extensions now to avoid damaging my own natural hair. As a result, I don't worry about dealing with roots or intensive treatments for my ends, instead I stick to a simple enough routine. I wash my hair every second day followed by a conditioner that hydrates it enough to not require a mask. Every second day I apply dry shampoo to soak up greasiness and add volume. If I'm styling my hair for a special occasion I'll use an oil, if I'm rushing out the door I'll use a beach spray and if my hair is up or curled I'll finish with hairspray. After years of trying and testing out different hair products it was only this year I stumbled across a brand that has become my all-time favourite. It was the story behind Kevin Murphy products that drew me in initially. He sourced companies that use micro cultivation, organic growing practices, and ecologically sound wild harvesting techniques to ensure the range is of the very highest natural quality. All of the hair products are sulphate, paraben and cruelty free, the packaging is unique. Not to mention, all of the products smell divine and most importantly they perform.

My TOP 5 HAIR PRODUCTS

Angel Wash is my Holy Grail shampoo and conditioner of choice. The duo is a delicate recovery range for fine, dry or broken hair. The bottles are quirky, girly and contain soothing ingredients like milk protein, aloe and olive esters that gently protect the hair in a low foam formulation. If you're looking for products that cleanse your hair sufficiently without stripping, control frizz and nourish dry ends, then this set is savage.

Fresh Hair has fast become my favourite dry shampoo of all time. As a gym bunny, it's a product I can't live without. Deemed the ultimate dry cleanser for your hair, this not only removes excess oil, it creates body, removes odours with a pleasant scent and can be used throughout the ends of your hair for extra texture.

Young Again is my favourite leave-in treatment oil when my ends require some extra attention. Infused with bur oil and grape seed extract to counteract the oxidation and ageing process caused by heated tools. I apply this prior to styling and after my hair is dry if I want a gorgeous glossy finish.

Beach Resort Spray is an ideal on-the-go styling product. If I want to avoid using heat on my hair, then applying this through my towel dried mid lengths and ends is awesome. Ideal for fine and medium textured hair, it's a weightless hair thickener that can be used to recreate year-round beachy waves. Ingredients like honey, citrus and tangerine make your hair smell like holidays too.

Session Spray is a fabulous finishing product. Whether I'm looking to tame baby hairs when my hair is tied up or create long lasting curls, I lean towards this can. Containing weightless resins, it delivers a flexible finish and hold, sexy shine without stiffness. The spray smells nice without catching your breath and the large size lasts a long time.

Nails

From the age of 6 up until I was 18, I had the terrible habit of biting my nails, a nervous habit I picked up from my mum.

I had the most horrible chubby fingers. If I was excited or anxious my nails would suffer and I tried every tip and trick in a bid to banish the habit. From those vile tasting pots that stop you putting your hands in your mouth to getting acrylic and gel nails applied to prevent me from chewing my tips, I gave everything a go. After a few sets of gels I had them removed and my own nails had grown considerably underneath. I was so in awe of my natural nail length that I promised myself I would do everything in my power to finally kick the addiction once and for all. I invested in a nail hardener, which I applied every night before a new polish colour. For every week that went by that I didn't bite my nails, I would purchase a new polish as a reward. After building an extensive collection, my nails eventually became stronger and instead of biting them I set time aside to give myself regular manicures. No matter how stressed I am, now I never have the urge to nibble at my nails and they've remained relatively robust. Although I've continued to get square or stiletto nails, I've been leaning towards the more natural look of late and prefer a gel polish that lasts a couple of weeks. I find weight lifting too difficult with long nails and prefer the look of a clean, classic square manicure. I tend to go to my local salon for Shellac or Gelish on my hands and toes meaning I don't have to worry about chipped nails during the week and it's a quick and easy way to get pampered before a trip or travel with work.

My TOP 5
NAIL PRODUCTS

Morgan Taylor is my favourite three-step system. The Stick With It base coat is followed by a professional finish polish of your choice and sealed in place using the Make It Last top coat. I notice a massive difference in the finish and longevity of my mani when using these beauty buys.

Sally Hansen Miracle Gel is my favourite salon finish mani without the use of LED lights, just a high technology top coat you can apply yourself at home. This part-lacquer and part-gel manicure system promises to deliver up to 14 days of lasting colour and shine in just 2 easy steps. The finish is ultra glossy and the shade range is great.

The Body Shop Sweet Almond Oil is my all-time favourite nail polish remover. This product effectively removes all nail colour gently with this 4 in 1 caring formula. Infused with ingredients like sweet almond, soya oil and sugarcane essence it also smells lovely compared to most removers.

Hand Chemistry are the most innovative hand hydrators I've come across. Aside from the pretty packaging, when applied the lovely layer feels lavish on the skin and even remains in place under running water, creating a droplet effect as protective proof. There are Intense Youth Complex, Extreme Hydration Complex, and Hyaluronic Rich versions, with each wonderful product packing a punch.

Essence Quick & Easy Sponge is a nifty, nail care oil in a practical pot that pampers. Almond and argan oil provide plenty of moisture without leaving behind an oily film, meaning you can go about your business straight after application. Just pop your finger into the pot, turn it around and you're left with cared for cuticles.

Top To Toe

Nothing beats a bubble bath after a long and stressful day. Lighting your favourite candle, playing your favourite tunes, relaxing, unwinding and pampering yourself with delicious products.

At least once a week I make sure to preen and perfect my body, which is somewhat neglected during the rest of the week. Having soft, supple skin is one of the most sexy attributes a woman can have and every partner I've been with has always commented on my skin. Harsh weather and negligence can leave your skin unsightly; dry and flakey with little lumps at the back of the arms and dry elbows the most common concerns for most people. An all-over glow can bring confidence and even slim out your frame, so finding the right routine is imperative. Using a hydrating bath bomb or bubble bath will start off your treatment time on the right step. The soak will soften your

skin and prepare it for the following pamper procedures. Being in the bath makes exfoliating and hair removal much easier. Although I generally wax, there are some occasions I have to shave prior to a last minute modelling job. The hot water will raise the hairs making them easier to reach and exfoliating products will apply like a dream. I also like to use a body brush to improve circulation, in turn reducing the appearance of cellulite. While I wash I like to leave a face and hair mask on to multi task from top to toe. After everything is ready to rinse I take a quick post-bath shower to freshen up and finish off. Once I'm out of the bath I like to apply a thick moisturiser before bed so that it can really get to work on my skin. If your hands and feet are in need of some TLC, then applying a hand or foot cream followed by gloves and thick socks is brilliant. It not only locks in moisture but traps the product overnight so you benefit from every last ingredient.

My TOP 5 BODY PRODUCTS

Lush bath products are perfect for pampering. From bombs to melts they fizzle and sparkle in water, working on improving every skin concern. The bright colours and fun shapes brighten your mood and although they're highly fragranced they contain natural ingredients and are handmade.

Cocoa Brown Tough Stuff is the ultimate, affordable, award winning exfoliator. Whether you wear tan or simply want to get rid of rough areas this can be used on the feet, ankles, knees, elbows and hands. This removes tan without being too harsh for sensitive skin and the hot pink product belongs in every bathroom.

Kiehl's Creme De Corps is hands down the best body moisturiser I've ever tried. I constantly get asked what I use to achieve a luminous glow and this is it. Enriched with the finest skin nurturing ingredients including beta carotene, cocoa butter and sesame oil it leaves skin soft, smooth and gorgeously glossy.

Garnier Ultimate Beauty Oil is my Holy Grail, budget buy body oil. Enriched with 4 precious oils including argan, macadamia, almond and rose this fragranced formula perfects the skin, giving it a radiant look. Legs feel instantly smoother and softer and your preparatory creams can work their magic underneath.

The Body Shop Peppermint Intensive Foot Rescue is fabulous for feet in need of TLC. The divine scent cools, refreshes and combats odour and is ideal applied after a long day. This product can be used overnight to soften hard skin and rehydrates dry heels.

Tanning Tips

One of the most controversial topics of conversation on my social media accounts over the years has been about tan. I have naturally sallow, olive skin and as a result never wear fake tan.

I suppose because the average Irish skin type is fair, people are in disbelief when I go three shades darker after a few hours in the sun. In the past I've tried bottles in a bid to bronze but always prefer my own skin tone. Aside from dry oils and shimmers, I haven't worn tan in almost two years. During the depths of winter when I'm at my palest shade and have a modelling gig coming up I've had spray tans, but in general the shade I am is always natural.

When I was younger I was extremely dark, and took the sun immediately even with the high protection my mum applied. Aside from looking after my skin with the above beauty regime I'm a huge fan of sun protection and aftercare. I firmly believe with the right SPF products you can get the most from your tan, maintain your colour and prevent ageing. Wearing a high factor on your face is so significant and something you should consider year-round regardless of the weather. UVB rays are responsible for sunburn, while UVA year-round rays have more long term damaging effects, like wrinkling and premature ageing. Aside from sunburn and detrimental effects that show at a later date, there are other effects you can prevent with the right products. Dark spots and pigmentation are a huge concern for most women and tend to show on the face prior to the body because the skin is far more delicate. Once you've followed the important safe sun steps then post sun products can add life to your golden glow. I literally lash on creams whilst on holidays; I use after sun immediately after exposure and after my shower, I then use a nourishing body cream and follow up with an oil for dinner time. Layering products in this manner leaves the skin soft, supple and less likely to peel meaning your tan looks terrific. There's nothing better than a holiday hue, the colours you wear pop, your body looks more toned and imperfections are disguised.

My TOP 5 TANNING PRODUCTS

The Shiseido Wetforce range is rather wonderful. Providing powerful protection for your skin, this innovative protective veil actually becomes even more effective when it comes into contact with water or perspiration. It also includes skincare ingredients that prevent dryness, oxidation and damage to cells and DNA.

NUXE Sun stock some the most beautiful body product protection around; from their packaging, scent and quality I simply can't fault this flawless sun range. The low protection oil, for example, is enriched with extracts of sun and water flowers to moisturise and soothe the skin while protecting it from UVA/UVB rays.

Clarins UV Plus is the ultimate day screen multi protection, with an SPF 50 for the face it's a luxurious high factor essential. This complete multi purpose day screen offers protection against the harmful effects of UV rays, free radicals and pollution to help users to maintain a youthful, radiant and even complexion. The consistency is lightweight and it doesn't leave a white cast, which is essential for those holiday snaps.

NUXE Sun range comes up trumps again in terms of post-sun products. Their Refreshing After Sun Lotion has a sublime sorbet texture that soothes the skin and provides immediate moisture. The range is every inch luxurious in terms of packaging and smells glorious and contains an ingredient called carob powder, which prolongs tan for two weeks.

Cocoa Brown Golden Goddess is my skin shimmer must have for making the most of your tan. This dreamy dry oil can be used on your body and hair to nourish, repair and beautify and has a glorious tahitian gardenia scent. The iridescent golden particles illuminate without looking glittery and the product doesn't transfer on your clothes.

Conclusion

Irrespective of your weight, size or shape, looking after your body with beauty products has tons of benefits.

Women who look after their skin, hair and nails tend to have better self-esteem and body image. By showing self-love from the outside in, you're looking after the body you were blessed with and making an effort to make yourself feel and look good.

Have you ever lounged in bed, avoiding a shower, eating ice cream and crying into your pillow after a break up? Did you feel better or worse? I know the moment I freshen up and collect my thoughts, putting my emotion into action by doing something nice for myself, I feel immediately better. Even if applying products on autopilot takes your mind off certain stress in your life it's a positive progression.

Speaking of stress, the more you look after yourself from the outside in, the less superficial stress you endure and in turn boost your immune system. If you have an interview and you're looking and feeling confident then you're more likely to ace the meeting and get that job. Taking the time out at least once a day to pamper yourself is a treat that will work on the body and mind beyond your initial comprehension. Smelling nice, having silky hair or clear skin can give you a boost, make you feel feminine and ready to take on the day. I'm not claiming that having a beauty regime will get you a partner, job or house, but it will make you feel better about yourself and putting effort into how you feel will in turn bring happiness. Happiness attracts happiness so why not make every positive step towards living a lovely life?

Chapter **10**

Fillers and Filters

Internet Insecurities

In a world where social media is so prevalent and celebrities have become icons who the younger generations look toward for guidance, things have changed dramatically.

TV and magazines have been around for a very long time. Models, for as long as they have existed, have had a certain desired shape. Editing of images is frequently used to create perfect pictures and cosmetic surgery occurs frequently.

However, with a new wave of reality TV and online blogging stars emerging over the past few years, the average audience now has more 'average' relatable people to look up to. Anyone with a significant following online or social media status can have a large number of impressionable girls and boys who watch their every move. As a beauty and lifestyle blogger with a huge audience, I know what that pressure can feel like. One wrong admission or claim and you can lose loyalty or upset people. On the plus side, if you approach things in a positive, classy and mature manner you can help and guide said demographic down the right path.

Working as a model in an industry that's predominantly based on looks, it's so easy to compare yourself to others and fall into the insecurity trap. Even if you carry yourself with confidence, at some point in your career you're bound to feel a bit frumpy at a fashion shoot, too young or too old amongst others at an event or not pretty enough. The same can be said for girls sifting through Instagram looking at stunning selfies or beautiful bodies and wondering why they don't look the same.

Not Everything Is As it Seems

The important thing to point out here is that the majority of people only post what they want other people to see and perceive.

Similarly to how celebrities have PR agents who only leak information that will benefit their client's career, bloggers and everyday individuals post only their highlight reel; positive and pretty updates from their dreamy day shared in a bid to accrue likes, popularity or book jobs. We all know no one wants to see the boring paperwork we're doing in the office, the bills we're paying in the bank or our plain plate of messily displayed food.

An Instagram account is a creative outlet, one where people follow you because they like the aesthetic look or the content of your posts. If you bear this in mind you will be less likely to fall into the trap of comparison when looking at what other people post. Selfies have become a very regular and acceptable visual update, as a result we see more of people's faces and tend to admire them like art and pick them apart in equal measures. When anyone with online fame posts their face to the world, they're leaving it open to critique just like a fitness technique, quote or take away pizza. Some will admire and adore the look while others will slag and bash individual facial features. People will also ask questions and what may start out as 'What lipgloss are you wearing?' or 'What product did you use in your brows?' can become 'Did you get Botox?' and 'She's definitely had her lips done.'

A Step Too Far

There's a fine line here between a genuine question and a downright rude comment. People may follow you online because they feel like they know you personally and want to get to know you even better.

As a result, they often expect answers to all questions and instant replies, which is almost impossible for the blogger or poster in question when they have thousands of followers.

I'm of the opinion that you should think before you type. Ask yourself if you would say the same thing that you're about to say on Facebook or Instagram if you were making the comment or asking the question in real life, to the person's face? Just because you follow and admire someone's work doesn't mean they owe you answers to everything or have to share every single part of their private life. I feel people find it easier to become an online troll or bully because the laptop protects them and their identity somewhat.

I'll talk trolls in more depth at the end of this chapter but for the moment I'll say this. Whether you're commenting on a popular account belonging to a business woman who has carved her career through sharing her life online or following a girl next door who utilises social media as a hobby and an escape from her work place, you should remember that each individual who exists behind each account is in fact a human being with feelings. You know those things called notifications on your iPhone? Each and every compliment, comment, query, or remark made on a social media account is notified to the person behind the account. They get a a little buzz or beep every time someone has something to say about their latest post and it's relatively difficult to ignore. So let's get back to one of those invasive questions and my thoughts on aesthetic alterations, namely fillers.

Perfecting My Pout

With new procedure options and minor work becoming the norm, there are so many questions circulating about who's had what work done, what options are available and if anyone should be altering their face or body to begin with.

One of the questions I am most frequently asked both publicly and privately is about my lips. Luckily I was blessed with relatively full lips, thanks to my beautiful mama fairy. I have a good natural shape and defined cupid's bow. However, about three years ago I was at an event where they demonstrated a natural form of lip filler that could be used to balance out uneven lips, fill in the upper lip for a more pronounced pout or match the upper to lower lip size and visa versa. I've always had a larger, more pronounced lower lip, and although it never bothered me to the point where I was massively unhappy, I was always interested in having a fuller upper lip. I felt it would complement the rest of my facial features and generally make me happier about my appearance.

I wasn't familiar with the options available until that event and always assumed the decision to fill your lips was permanent and had copious amounts of side effects. I was scared of having a trout pout and getting a botch job that would ruin the face I have to live with for the rest of my life. After doing extensive research, asking a whole host of questions and watching a demonstration on the procedure, I decided this kind of lip filler would suit me perfectly. I wasn't miserable about my face, I didn't hate my lips, I simply wanted to enhance the lips I had and fill my upper lip slightly to match my full lower lip. I made that decision at the age of 25; adult enough to be decisive, and mature enough to really think things through and weigh up the pros and cons. I think age is hugely important if you're interested in getting ANY serious treatment carried out.

Doing What's Right For You

This chapter is certainly not about suggesting that you need to ever consider having any changes made to your appearance, this goes for everything from waxing your body or choosing to wear make up to getting Botox or a boob job, the choice must be your own.

And this chapter is about just that, making it clear that every choice you make in life is YOUR choice. No one else has the right to judge or comment on your decisions and if you're making an educated, well thought through, safe decision that's going to make you happier throughout the life you choose to lead, then so be it. I'm a firm believer that once you're not harming yourself or upsetting anyone around you then your decision can't be all that bad.

Aside from my lips, I've never had any other work done, bar regular, skincare-based facial and body treatments. If, in the future, I decide to look into the likes of Botox, then that's something I will do in the same informed manner.

After having the lip filler procedure a handful of times now, I can say I'm very happy I made the initial decision and I'm extremely happy with my perfected pout. I find the finished look suits my facial features exactly as I envisaged it would and I've experienced no issues or regrets. If lip fillers are something you're looking into, I can only point you in the right direction and discuss my experience. The first step is choosing an aesthetician who is a known professional and who is extremely proficient in the area you're looking to explore. This step is so important; please do not skimp on money when it comes to such an important consideration. Once you've decided on your chosen clinic, I would advise a consultation where you can run through your desires and listen to the doctor's advice when it comes to what will best suit your face.

My Experience With Fillers

For my lips, I've been going to Clinical Nurse Specialist Marsha Harmon at ClearSkin clinic. With over 15 years of international experience, Marsha is an expert in the area of facial injections as well as medical grade skin care for acne and ageing skin.

Marsha has treated thousands of patients and regularly attends aesthetic conferences and academies around the world where top doctors and nurses in the industry present the latest trends, technologies, research and training on cosmedical and anti-ageing procedures.

When you walk into a clinic you want to feel at ease, it also has to be extremely hygienic and offer an array of professional services and certificates. You must also feel at ease with your doctor; a warm, friendly and professional relationship should be built where trust is gained and above all you feel in safe hands. I also think it's important that whoever you're dealing with is both blunt and honest with you. You may have a visual idea in your head of what you want to achieve but that may not be feasible or suit you personally. It's therefore a good idea to bring in an example celebrity lip shape as a guide but bear in mind, their lips are not yours and the outcome won't be the same so you can't expect exact results. A trained professional is there to guide you and refuse to do anything that would harm or hinder your appearance. ClearSkin and Marsha tick all of these boxes for me. In my case, I had the likes of Lana Del Rey in mind because her nose and mouth are very similar to mine and it's known that she gets lip fillers done, so I felt it was an ideal comparison. Marsha refused to go as big as Lana for fear my nose would tip slightly and my lips would look too fake, so I accepted the advice and agreed.

Frequently Asked Questions

Moving onto the procedure itself, I'm not going to lie and pretend the experience isn't painful, using any form of injection whether it's to numb an area or inject filler is going to hurt somewhat, it just depends on your pain threshold.

At ClearSkin, they use hyaluronic acid based dermal lip fillers. This is a very safe product as hyaluronic acid is a natural substance found in the body and is very unlikely to cause an allergic reaction. Hyaluronic acid fillers also give greater control over lip volume and have reasonably long-lasting results.

After each consultation prior to treatment I discuss the shape and volume I'm after. Because I've been getting the treatment for the past couple of years now it's generally a top up in my case. Following a consultation, the lips are cleaned and numbed with a topical anaesthetic. A small amount of product is injected into the lips, little by little, as Marsha continually checks the shape. You can watch the whole procedure in a mirror and see instant results, which is great and allows more control. The procedure takes approximately 15 minutes and the results last approximately 6 months. This depends on each individual and how they break down the product, it also depends on how many times you've had the procedure before as a small amount of product will always remain.

Being Professional About My Pout

The reason why I chose to discuss this topic in my book is because I felt the subject needed to be addressed.

On almost every selfie I have posted during the past year, someone has commented about my lips, either complimenting me on their shape or asking if they are natural, so I feel it's time to clear the air.

So many women and men have thin lips and would love for them to be more full without making a permanent change to their pout. Having my upper lip filled with a small amount of product that my body naturally breaks down every few months is the ideal solution for me because it is an educated choice I made at the right age, for the right reasons and with the right surgeon.

However, answering followers publicly on social media about this issue, using short sentences and the limited space available, did not seem acceptable in my eyes. It is a serious topic and deserves to be dealt with in the proper forum, such as here, with thought out information. With a young demographic of impressionable followers and mothers alike, I never wanted to condone or suggest anyone getting their lips done without being able to tell my full story, so I always avoided the subject. I am a role model and I take that position very seriously. I never lied, I simply avoided addressing the subject for professional reasons. If anyone was downright rude about my lips or caused controversy I simply deleted the comment to avoid the volcano effect. If a girl politely emailed me privately about my lips or asked me in person, I always answered them in a lengthy educated manner with suggestions of the top Irish lip doctors to contact.

At the end of the day, being in the spotlight will always attract curiosity, there just has to be a certain limit to what you share and how you share it. I personally don't feel the need to tell the world about my lip fillers under a make up selfie and I don't feel that I owe anyone an answer, but this book allowed me an avenue of expression that is hopefully helpful, insightful and above all informative. It's unfortunate that something like this is so sensationalised and not seen as a private cosmetic decision, but with a wave of lip plumping lip glosses available and women sucking on tools to enlarge their lips, it seems to be a very popular topic of discussion. Thanks Kylie.

The Art of Editing

In this chapter I also wanted to discuss photography all the way from taking the initial snap to the fine art of editing and filters.

From iPhone apps to full on Photoshop, I think I've managed to become quite proficient in the art of editing. Whenever I hold my workshops around Ireland, one of the most frequently asked questions is about how I take and edit my pictures. So many of you have a keen interest in photography and want to improve your finished product without going to college to study the subject. There are also so many make up artists out there trying to make a living and utilise social media to the maximum, meaning their feed has to be filtered and on fleek. A poor quality photograph can make your clients look haggard and your work look rubbish. A great pic, by the same token, can gain you hundreds of new followers and bookings, so it's important to educate yourself in this area and get creative. Although I went to art college and have always been prolific in this area, I never actually studied photography. I always loved taking pictures;

capturing the perfect moment, printing memories from holidays or nights out with friends and saving them in sparkly handmade scrapbooks. When technology took an advanced turn I was overjoyed at the improved phone camera quality and social media sharing options. Images are not only an instant visual, they can tell a story or portray a professional situation far better than text. Nowadays people's attention spans are short; everyone wants things immediately and file sharing has meant followers can scroll through a feed that inspires everything from their food and fitness to their shopping list and style.

Social Media Savvy

I'm practically obsessive compulsive when it comes to organising and a nit-picker by nature. From the very beginning I was a perfectionist when it came to The Make Up Fairy.

I would never post a blurry, out of focus image, I thought about the layout of objects I was photographing, I also put the same efforts into images of myself in a bid to showcase the most flattering poses and dainty duck faces. I spend as much time taking an image of my nails for a beauty product post as I do my outfit details or animals. Photography is a hugely enjoyable outlet for me and I love playing around with editing and filters in my free time. It's also very much a part of what I do for my brand, meaning there's an added importance and pressure on us beauty and lifestyle bloggers. No one wants bad photos to be posted online and considering I am my brand, outstanding photo quality and a varied feed is, in my eyes, integral.

Two other essential ingredients, originality and diversity, are key when it comes to your feed. People don't want to see ten quotes in a row or the same pair of runners 20 times in one day. Your days will vary and some will be more exciting than others but ensuring your images are high quality and that the editing is of a high standard means you don't need to worry as much about the chosen content or frequency, you just need to have a certain amount of consistency. When you're consistent people know when to expect an upload, become addicted to your feed and hungry for more.

Tools and Tricks of the Trade

I'm a huge fan of Apple and have always taken the majority of my online images with an iPhone. I currently work with an iPhone 6 and adore the quality and shooting options.

In terms of my professional blog imagery, I use a Canon DSLR 650D, which was an investment when I became serious about my website. As a blogger and YouTuber I wanted a camera with combined quality and functionality for both shooting and filming and this baby is one of the best on the market. The creative auto function is fantastic for beginners and pretty much fool proof. If you're starting a blog, the best thing you can do is allocate a budget for equipment and give some time to learning how to use it. Whether it's a good phone or professional camera it will immediately improve the standard of your online presence.

Taking photos of yourself and practising poses is an excellent way to get to know your angles and become familiar with the buttons and options. If you have a family member or friend at home, show them the shooting manual and ask them to take some pictures for you. The process of taking images, uploading them, deciding which ones make the final cut and the post edit is the same process that a professional photographer goes through and can be self-taught to a certain extent, depending on what you need the images for.

A tripod is the next natural investment. A tripod will allow you to take images when no one else is around and stabilise the camera for the likes of filming. It's hard to rely on someone else to take your images, especially when they're not in the same industry, so this is the perfect independent alternative. Next stop is lighting. I generally work with natural daylight where possible for taking images and filming, but I also have two soft box lights, which give a studio standard to your work and flawless finish. Lots of YouTubers also use a Diva Ring, which is a less cumbersome piece of equipment that's just as good and easier to fit in smaller spaces. When I'm taking pictures I'll choose an option that suits whatever I'm taking imagery of. For example, if I'm taking images of flowers from far away, then the landscape option may work well. The same goes for lighting; when taking product imagery the auto flash function is generally perfect and for make up shots and beauty shots daylight or softbox lighting is preferable.

The Art of the Selfie

I recently saw a very appropriate meme for this chapter. 'Sure there are so many bigger problems in the world than girls who think they are pretty. One of those problems is girls who don't think they are pretty'.

If taking a good selfie makes you feel more confident and happier for the day, then why not get good at it. At this point in my career, I think I've successfully managed to master the art of the selfie. I know the angles to use to make myself appear slimmer or more curvy, I know how to get the best lighting to hide blemishes, and enhance the end result so that my image is picture perfect for posting. To begin with, find the largest window in your house with the most natural daylight, obviously during the day is the only time suitable for this type of selfie. Natural daylight is the most flattering for the face and reduces the requirement for post-editing of images. This type of lighting will make your eye colour and make up pop, your skin look clear and bright and your overall look most organic.

As an experiment, try taking a selfie in front of a window followed by the exact same selfie in artificial bathroom lighting. Big difference, right? The former can be a confidence boost and the latter can make you second guess your appearance. The yellow tinge from most artificial bulbs will make you appear older by highlighting flaws and wrinkles and even deepening your under eye bags and circles. If you want to take a selfie at night from home and have invested in soft box lighting, my suggestion is to allow the bulb to heat up, place it about five feet away from you and voilà, studio standard selfie from your bedroom.

Know Your Angles

Learning how to pose and knowing your angles is just as important as your lighting.

If you take an image from above with your camera lens facing down, you will naturally look slimmer. Therefore the opposite also applies, if you take an image from below head level you will automatically add at least ten pounds. You know that terrifyingly unexpected front facing camera? The one that showcases the nine chins you didn't realise you had? That's the angle that should be kept solely for funny Snapchats, ain't no body got time for that on social media. My signature stance is an image taken from above, with my head slightly tilted to the left, pointing my head down. This angle flatters my face, showcasing my best features like my cheekbones and jawline and slims my overall appearance. I will either make my eyes wide and bright, giving an innocent appearance, or slightly narrowed, making Tyra Banks proud about my 'smizing' abilities, which gives a more sultry, sexy look. In terms of full body poses, the generic tea pot pose is so popular because it flatters most figures. Not only does it angle your arm, pulling your limbs out away from your body creates a more flattering silhouette and defines your waist. Placing your hand on your hip will actually guide in your love handles and will also create more a more toned appearance in the likes of a bikini shot on holidays, hey presto baby, abs.

Curated Content

When you're happy with your selection of selfies, narrow them down to your top three picks.

I tend to keep the best image for my initial make up and hair update on social media, the second for details of everything I'm wearing and to answer questions followers have and the third for a latergram on a day when I'm at home looking like a hot mess and have nothing pretty to post.

Now to the fun part, editing. Not everyone agrees with or likes photo editing, just like the fillers we discussed earlier in this chapter, filters aren't going to be to everyone's taste, but I'm all for a good Valencia. Filters and creative editing can make your feed really stand out from the thousands of others within an already saturated industry, and make your brand become unique and artistic. I'm asked daily what editing apps and filters I use to achieve the images I post and I've kept them secret until now. I never hid the fact I used apps or filters, I just wanted my accounts to be different and if I told everyone what I used then my feed would become too generic and similar to everyone else's.

If I want a particular light effect, for example, I research what app would be suitable, I also always keep on top of trending apps and look up the popular suggestions for font and image overlay options. I keep a folder on my phone for editing that has about 18 different apps inside but I always return to the same favoured ones. I've compiled my Top 5 for you all including why I love them so much and how I use them.

My TOP 5 APPS

GIMP I don't actually own Photoshop but a friend suggested GIMP when I first started blogging and I've relied on it ever since for laptop and desktop editing. This is the only app on my list that isn't used on phones, but perfect for those of you who work on images from your computer. The programme is free and has all the basic editing elements of Photoshop. A versatile graphic manipulation package, there's a customisable interface and tons of photo enhancement options. GIMP is ideal for digital retouching, has brilliant hardware support and lots of online tutorials to get you started, it will also save you a lot of money.

Moldiv Moving onto phone apps, the first thing I suggest you download is some form of photomontage app. My preferred pick is Moldiv which lets you combine and edit multiple images to make amazing collages. The app has fantastic frames and lots of other photo editing options, effects, filters and decoration features like text captions and numerous stamps. I personally love using this app for events, food pictures and outfit posts because it allows me to include a few visuals in one update.

Afterlight If you're interested in producing professional high quality photos, this app is one of the most versatile around. From scenery to selfies, there's a selection for everyone. With a wide variety of advanced options including clarify, contrast, saturation, hue, lights and shadows, filters, light leaks, overlays and brilliant borders, this app will really make your images eccentric.

Facetune The Holy Grail selfie editor, Facetune is the most popular app amongst all big name beauty gurus and celebrities. Described as the fun and powerful portrait editor, this app will help you achieve magazine-like results. From skin smoothing to defining details you can perfect everything from making your eyes pop and teeth dazzle to blurring backgrounds and even removing blemishes. I always use this app for my selfies especially ones where make up or an accessory is the key focal point.

ABM Also known as A Beautiful Mess this is the ultimate girly app for adding beautiful borders, delightful doodles and text tools. You can begin by choosing a wacky wallpaper and colourful collage and complete your edit with floral borders, ready-made phrases or wording of your choice. Brilliant for bloggers, this app is also a fun way to pass some time and get creative.

Handling Hate

When you've created your own personal online space whether it's as a blogger who writes about body image, a mum who's interested in poetry, a teen who's using social media to connect with school pals or a girl boss looking to make it big on Instagram, you must protect your positive space.

I really despise the word 'hater' but it's become such a common way to describe online bullies and trolls. When you open yourself up to a following you are also exposing yourself to negativity and for every ten nice comments there's a strong possibility that one nasty comment will affect you the most. We simply can't avoid criticism in this world and everyone is entitled to varied opinions. Unfortunately not everyone has the social etiquette or respect to express critique in the nicest way. Trust me, I've experienced a certain level of negativity in my time, from the real world and online. Thankfully I've learned to brush it off, utilise it to my advantage and hopefully handle it in a polite and positive manner.

The first piece of advice I can give you is not to take anything personally, as difficult as that sounds. From compliments to criticism, try not to let either get in your head; an inflated ego or scorned bitchy persona are both equally unattractive. You must appreciate your followers whether they're family members you love, friends you care about or random people who found your page and admire you. No matter how busy I am, I always try to get back to everyone's comments, whether it's to thank and offer appreciation, answer a query or address negativity.

I pride myself on maintaining a level of professionalism mixed with approachability, and it's worked considerably well for me so far.

Protect Your Online Space

If you're experiencing negativity online there are a few methods I can suggest for handling the situation. If someone is bullying you or being unnecessarily rude and nasty there's a lovely little block button.

There's enough negativity in this life that we don't need to endure actual and completely uncalled for vitriol. If a comment upsets you when you look at it but you don't want to be extreme and block someone, the delete comment option is also available. I have wasted so much time feeling down about insignificant observations because I refused to delete comments, now I see my space as just that, MINE, and the way I see it is if a commenter is just there to be negative then I don't need to see it or allow it affect my day.

If someone brings up a valid point that can be deemed negative but expresses it in an educated and kind manner, I will always respond in a similar fashion. Retorting to a comment you dislike with a rude attitude will only open you up to even more negativity, fuel fire in someone who wants to start an argument or actually upset someone who was simply making a point. Try and remember that most people online don't actually know you in person so nothing they say should affect you, the people who truly matter know who you are, have admired your heart and soul and spent time with the genuine good person you are. We all portray a certain persona online and if you try and treat that persona like an alter ego that has a fabulous sparkle shield, protecting you from all harm, you won't be affected as much by what people might say anymore. If someone doesn't like my eyebrows or bum, for example, I'll reply with a cheeky thank you. If they don't like my new fitness regime, that's fine they don't have to do it. If, however, they are obnoxious about someone else, wrongly accuse me of something or slate my business then I'm proactive and protective, I might post a well-written rant or long winded reply.

Spreading the Love

To conclude, the most important filler in your life should be happiness and with that comes the ability to filter out negativity. If something is really bothering you my best advice is to take at least ten minutes out to do or focus on something else.

If it's no longer bothering you when you return, fantastic you've moved on. If it's still bothering you then take some deep breaths and think before you type. If you respond immediately you run the risk of sounding scorned and aggressive and it can have a domino effect where lots of other followers get involved and feelings are hurt. When you take the time out to collate your argument you'll have a better chance of articulating your point in a courteous manner.

Keeping a beautiful bit of bubble wrap around your online space is beyond important, so knowing how to handle various situations that may arise is paramount. If you're one of my younger readers be sure to speak to an adult if you're experiencing any form of online bullying or upset. People around you are there to listen and help remove the weight from your shoulders. Similarly if you're in an older more mature demographic but in a vulnerable place in your life, share your fears and worries with someone. We all know what having a bad day is like and a negative comment online can be the tip of the iceberg. The more conscious we are that every online profile has a person behind it, the happier the internet can be. A wonderful tool that's created so many jobs and education for so many people, we need to treat the space with the same respect we would in a classroom or office. Technology is constantly advancing and we need to move forward with grace and approbation in order to enjoy this creative outlet.